BEYOND SALES

50 BUSINESS PROBLEMS EVERY CEO NEEDS TO SOLVE

GENE NAFTULYEV

NAFTULYEV, LLC

Roy H Williams - for his guidance
Brad Whittington - for his motivation
Erik Moon - for his copious critique and feedback
Mark Anthony Bates - for his encouragement
Mike Koenigs - for his friendship

FOREWORD

I first heard of Gene Naftulyev from Daniel Whittington.

Daniel had somehow wrangled himself an invitation to an exclusive New Year's dinner with a group of business tycoons at which the host, Gene Naftulyev, decided to paint his portrait.

It is an amazing work of art.

A few weeks later, Gene showed up in a class I was teaching on Practical Applications of Chaos Theory. I knew he wasn't just a painter when he began asking questions.

You can learn everything you need to know about a person by the questions they ask.

No, that isn't entirely true; you can't learn what they do for a living.

Fascinated by his intellect, I asked Gene about his business during a break in the class. He handed me his card. Beneath his name was the phrase "Legitimate Business Man." I laughed, of course, and Gene smiled. It didn't seem appropriate to press the matter further, so I dropped it.

A few days later, I learned that Gene had signed up for every other class we teach and donated the money to build our now-famous Whiskey Vault. Gene's commitment of time and money to our school was impressive.

"Daniel, what does Gene do for a living?"

"Well, he... uh..." Daniel paused and looked puzzled for a moment, then his eyes met mine as he said, "I'm not really sure."

I spent 2 or 3 days a month with Gene for the next 18 months as he attended all our 2 and 3-day classes and workshops, and at the end of that time, I still had no idea what Gene Naftulyev did for a living. Every person who met Gene liked and admired him, but not one of them could tell me what he did for a living.

I had experienced this once before. It was 1998. My publisher called to say he had been sent a copy of a bookstore receipt indicating that someone had purchased 500 copies of my book, The Wizard of Ads, and on that receipt was scribbled the note, "Is this enough for you to arrange for me to meet the author?"

The publisher, Ray Bard, asked, "Are you willing to do it?"

Intrigued, I said, "Sure, why not?"

A couple of weeks later I spent a delightful day with Dean Rotbart. After he had left for the airport at the end of the day, Pennie asked, "So what does Dean do?"

Puzzled, I said, "I'm not sure. I can tell you that his wife is named Talya, and his children are Maxwell and Avital, and they have a very happy family." Thinking back to the previous several hours, it dawned on me that every time I had asked

Dean about his business, he had skillfully deflected my question with one of his own.

He kept me talking about me.

A few weeks later, Pennie and I received a mysterious invitation to attend a black tie gala in the Grand Ballroom at the Waldorf-Astoria in New York. Seated at the head table between Dean Rotbart and Paul Steiger, the managing editor of The Wall Street Journal, in a room of 1,000 important journalists dressed in tuxedos and evening gowns, we were frightened out of our wits. It was when Lou Dobbs and Maria Bartiromo – the Masters of Ceremonies – stepped up to the microphone that the mystery of Dean's identity was finally solved.

Dean Rotbart had been a legendary investigative reporter for The Wall Street Journal and this party was an annual event hosted by him to spotlight journalists he felt to be worthy of special recognition. Receiving a TJFR award from Dean Rotbart was almost like winning a Pulitzer Prize.

Who else but a skillful investigative reporter could so easily keep you talking about yourself while telling you nothing at all about them self?

Gene Naftulyev, that's who.

Gene isn't a journalist, but he is most definitely an investigator.

I was talking to a friend who employs about 250 people in 3 different companies when he mentioned that he had hired a specialist to figure out what was wrong with a company that was underperforming.

"Who did you hire?"

"A fellow named Gene Naftulyev."

Eureka!

"He's going to figure out what's holding you back?"

"Yeah. He's famous for it."

"How famous?"

"Procter & Gamble. American Express. Kraft Foods. Target. They're all clients of Gene's."

"What does he do, exactly?"

"He improves profits without spending money."

"But how?"

"Process re-engineering, operational optimization, making business units autonomous, negotiating employee and consultant contracts and a hundred other things like that. It just depends on what you need. He refines the core of your business so that you become more efficient, have fewer frustrations and make more money. Naftulyev can always spot the problems and his fixes are famously quick and easy."

"Hello?"

"Gene, this is Roy Williams. I want to talk to you about writing a book."

"Why?"

"Because I'd like to read it."

There was a long pause at the other end of the line. Then Gene said, "Okay, I'll do it."

This is that book.

You can thank me later.

Roy H. Williams

Author of the New York Times bestselling Wizard of Ads trilogy,

Founder, Wizard Academy

PREFACE

I wrote this book because most business advice I read is a rehash of stale conventional wisdom.

I wrote this book because my friend Roy Williams challenged me to write it.

I wrote this book to expose more people to the UNCON-VENTIONAL business thinking that I use with my clients to solve their fundamental business problems.

This book will piss some people off. Roy says that is a good thing!

Just so you know, I use the terms founder, owner, and CEO somewhat interchangeably, not because they are the same, but because for most of this book the advice applies equally regardless of the which of those roles you fill. When there is a need for a distinction between founder and CEO, I will make it very clear.

I will strive to do my best to straddle the line between detailing real stories of business problems and keeping my clients information as confidential today as the day I signed my confidentiality agreements. Some of the stories go back 20 years and technically are no longer confidential. However, I believe I can provide the gist of the situation without getting into the specifics to the extent that the client is readily identifiable.

My intent in all cases is not to point out what was bad about the company or that what they did that was wrong, but instead to learn from the experience and show how best to solve that problem.

A few people who read the draft of this book asked for more details of how I helped solve each of these problems. If you find yourself seeing your own situation in these pages and want to find out more details about a specific solution, please jump to the last chapter which contains my contact information. If I were to include the detailed steps to every single solution discussed in the book, this would be a 2000 page book, rather than 200! So if you get enough guidance on your own - great! But if you need additional help, please go to the last chapter.

Lastly, if you are a past client reading this and are assuming the story is about you, it probably isn't about your company. It's amazing how many of my clients think their problems are unique!

I

BIG PICTURE

CLARIFY AND IMPLEMENT VISION OF CEO

PRESCRIPTIVE, NOT REACTIVE

*W*hen asked, most business founders say something like "I try to stay true to the vision I had when I started the company." Are you inclined to answer that question the same way? What if you ask a few of your employees that question? For bonus points: What if you ask your customers?!

The reality is that just about everyone stops thinking and communicating about their vision shortly after hiring the fifth employee. How do I know this, I've asked the employees in companies I've worked with, and the only ones who recall the vision being communicated clearly to the staff are employees 1-5.

But wait, does that mean that there is no vision? Or just that employees are not aware of it? Let me answer that question with a question. If employees are your most significant cost center, and you hire them to do the things that make the company grow and prosper, then how can they do their jobs while not knowing the vision of the CEO?

Clarifying and implementing the vision is one of the most significant areas I've seen leaders fail, in both companies large and small. Developing a vision is essential, and there have been countless books written on that topic. People who call themselves business coaches often focus on developing a business vision with the CEO. Marketing leadership usually has to weave the business vision into the branding and advertising of a company. Companies without vision fail at a much higher rate than ones who take the time and effort to define a vision. But that is just step one!

The follow up to having a well-developed vision is to be able to clarify that vision in a way that all your employees can move the company to closer alignment with that vision. Clarifying your vision is in a sense translating it for each department and then each role in the organization. If the vision is to sell the best titanium bolt at a reasonable price, then each person in the company from the executive assistant, to the HR manager, to the machinist needs to understand how their role can affect the company vision. They also need to understand what factors they need to be focused on while interacting with other workers in the company to best make the vision a reality. It may be about the cost to the accounting department, not the purity of the raw material to the Engineering team. In fact, it is about different things to different groups, and while long-term employees generally gain an understanding of their role in creating the best product, they do this without a formal process of clarification and validation.

Your employees (including contractors) are the people who will implement your vision. Leaving your employees without an understanding of company vision will reduce their chance of success and require more management interaction.

Sometimes employees only see a part of your vision. There are many companies I've worked with who have demonstrated the dangers of not correctly communicating their vision. One company I worked with, in particular, had a vision of creating millionaires out of users of their products. But it had no mechanism inside the company to make that happen consistently. The result was that customers felt unsupported after purchasing their products because they bought into the vision of the company as customers, but the company did not clarify that message to their employees. Employees heard the message but were not provided tools or a direction of how to accomplish that vision. Everyone just did what they thought was their job as well as they could. This created both frustrations for the customers and stress for the CEO at having frustrated customers. The solution, in this case, was to create a new testing and certification department for the customers. People felt much better when they were being challenged to learn and then be tested on their knowledge of the skills they learned. Only when the company vision was clarified did it become apparent that to implement that vision the company needed to create a way to challenge and test their clients. Much like a personal trainer helps more than just an exercise program, so in this case were clients better able to achieve financial growth.

Of course, it didn't hurt the company to create another revenue stream!

SPECIALIZED SKILL RECRUITMENT

HOW TO FIND THAT PERFECT PERSON

*I*n my last book, I talked about differences in both the types of employees and even executives that a company needs throughout its growth and maturation. So here is a summary of that chapter from my previous book.

For many entrepreneurs, the traditional wisdom is that if you do a good job hiring at the early stages of business, you only have to hire someone for a position once and they will grow with the company. I will get into why people think there is never a need to replace anyone, and why that is wrong in a later chapter, but let me focus on the hiring process itself in this chapter. Hiring the right people means you need to avoiding hiring the wrong people, and there are many ways to hire the wrong people.

For instance during those early employee hires, you need to be sure you hire for flexibility and trainability. Everyone, you included, has to wear a lot of different hats. The company can't afford to hire experts to fill each need yet. Even the owners are probably not experts; rather, they are simply willing to pick up whatever needs to get done to make the next sale and do it.

If successful through the initial startup, what you want to end up with several years later is:

- Written procedures and processes in place.
- A management team that plans and knows how to minimize unplanned events.
- Expertise in their departments who work with other experts in other departments.
- No one is a jack of all trades anymore.

The personal challenge you face as the CEO - and that the rest of the CxO management team face - is being OK with not knowing the up to the minute operational details of the company the way you used to. Your focus is on guiding an ever-growing organization, which means, much like a conductor of an orchestra, you focus on what will be happening next, rather than what is happening now. You trust your management staff to execute on the future plans and keep you informed enough to be able to make right strategic decisions. They, in turn, trust their department heads to know enough about day-to-day, but not necessarily minute-by-minute operations.

The most important reason to hire someone is that they have skills which a company needs, are willing to utilize those skills when the company needs them, and are eager to do this at a rate the company can afford. Secondary qualities, like people skills, will help determine how well this person fits into the company culture and how effectively they will interact with employees already at the company are also important. However, you as a founder or a senior manager liking someone as a person, while it is obviously a plus, should be much lower on the list.

I have been able to find very good people to hire for my clients, but that is not an easy process. Finding a great employee means the company has to do as much work as the person applying for a job. What I mean by that is great hires do not stay available for long. You may receive 25 resumes and see five great potential hires, but those five may have sent out resumes to 25 companies, and the first company to interview them and give them an offer is likely to get them. So do not waste time with filtering tactics that make the candidates jump through hoops. Instead set up an interview immediately with anyone who's resume looks impressive. The first interview may be only 15 minutes and cover just a few questions, but at that point they are not likely to take another offer without talking to you first. If you simply email your candidates a list of questions, and other companies are already setting up interviews, guess what your odds are of getting a reply to your email?

If you take too long from initial contact to an interview, you will simply end up with the candidates who are most desperate, not the ones who may be the best fit. Finding the perfect employee is easy - it just takes the same amount of effort as making the perfect product or delivering the perfect service!

For many CEOs I've worked with, hiring people is second only to firing people as the least enjoyable part of the job in the company. Even 'people' people from sales and marketing departments dislike spending time to find the best candidates. Unfortunately very often that means the solution is just to hire the first person who comes along, replies to filter questions, and doesn't blow the interview just so they can end the hiring process. This leads to a company full of mediocre people doing an OK job. No one is terrible, but it also means it doesn't take much to stand out in this crowd.

The TV show The Office was based on following the fictional lives of mediocre people selling a boring product. In that show no one is motivated to do more than the bare minimum. While the head of the office constantly comes up with ideas to motivate people but accomplishes nothing but distracting them from their work. The show was funny precisely because it showed an office full of people doing mediocre work and a boss who thought that his staff was great. It was a TV show written by utterly NOT mediocre comedy writers!

Another common occurrence is to see a company full of twenty-somethings. Yes, there certainly are examples of companies started by teens and others staffed by people just starting their professional careers, like Facebook in its early days, but let's face it, a successful company like that is a unicorn - it just doesn't happen very often. For most businesses that have an age bias in either direction, this is a detriment to the success of the company as it starts growing past a half dozen employees. Youth can have skill and energy, but if not balanced with wisdom, which only comes from making mistakes - maybe lots of mistakes - it does not provide the best workforce long term. Likewise a company full of very experienced people will be missing the energy and creativity of inexperience which often leads to completely out-of-the-box solutions to problems.

I'm a fan of using interns precisely because they bring something unique to the workforce which cannot be taught - namely, an unbiased view of existing processes. But unless you are in college, and you don't know anyone over 25, you really should be hiring some of your people based on experience and the wisdom it brings to balance out the exuberant enthusiasm of youth. Certainly, by the time you hire your 5th or 10th employee, you should be recruiting for skill and experience.

Mistakes can be made by everyone. Your goal in hiring more seasoned and specialized staff is to pay for what they learned from past mistakes through a higher salary or hourly rate. You pay for more inexperienced staff mistakes through unexpected business losses that come at the most inopportune times when a business follows through on a bad decision.

How do I find the best people if I don't like wasting time on the hiring process? Well if you can afford to use recruiters (15-25% of annual salary) then do so, but only after doing due diligence on the recruiter. Don't just trust someone who paid $9.99 for a business card with the word "Recruiter" to help you find a person who will be responsible for potentially millions of dollars in profits or losses for your company. Have the recruiter audition for you. Have them explain their process for finding the best employee for you. Have them tell you about their successes as well as failures of the past. Tell them you want to use one recruiter for the next five years, so they are potentially going to make hundreds of thousands off your company, and that you want to be sure that is the kind of relationship they bring to the table. If you can find a good recruiter, you can avoid having to find new employees on your own. If you can't find a good recruiter, then don't use a recruiter as they will merely cost you money and solve none of the problems that you would have if you just hired poorly yourself.

After the initial startup period of hiring generalists, one of the skills of a successful CEO is being able to surround himself with people that are more qualified than he is at their particular specialization. Look around your company and think about the people who you see as being better than you. For each one, you can honestly say that about - congratulations, you made a good hire. For everyone else in roles which are specialized, you probably need to start looking for their replacement sooner than later. For menial or entry level roles you should not expect that people know more than you about doing that job, but they should at least be faster, more efficient, or more regimented in doing their jobs than you would be if you had to do it yourself.

Any fault with the staff within a company always rolls up through management and executives to the CEO. Find good specialists, set high expectations for their hires, and you will have a company of the top producers in your industry. Shrug off the responsibility to take the time to hire the best of the best, and your bottom line will suffer.

I had one client that had shown an ability to grow sales very quickly. They were riding the wind as it were. Then it turned out that ride was unsustainable. When I came in, I was surprised to find a company full of people in their 20s. I wondered if it was all the innovative ideas of younger employees that helped them grow so fast. It may have been, but it was also the cause of their downfall. As I mentioned, everyone makes mistakes, as much as we try to be perfect. We can make fewer mistakes by remembering our own past errors and the mistakes of others. Nothing will prevent someone from making an error in judgment nearly as much as a bitter memory of the price they paid the last time they made the same mistake.

Learning from others' mistakes is a half-step in the right direction, and it contains wisdom, but not the instruments of enforcing adherence to that wisdom. So when you have a company staffed by people who have made very few business mistakes in their lives, they will not help you as the CEO in avoiding mistakes. They have nothing to fall back on personally, and they will respect and admire you as the successful CEO even if you make bad decisions, further hurting your decision-making abilities by creating a false sense of always being right. We see this type of thing happen with politicians all the time. They surround themselves with sycophants and then end up falling from grace, but never understanding why they fall so far.

Making mistakes is human, learning from your own mistakes and the mistakes of others makes you superhuman. Unfortunately most people need to make the same mistake multiple times before they actually learn from it. For companies that is often even worse because mistakes get institutionalized and become part of the normal process. It's not wisdom unless you avoid the same mistake in the future

If you have no other reason than this to surround yourself

with people who are more experienced and better qualified than you, it is that their internal criticism and disagreements with you will give you the opportunity to prevent making extremely costly mistakes with the entire company. But that will only happen if you take their advice!

If you surround yourself with only enthusiastic but inexperienced youngsters, they will have little criticism to offer you and you will keep making costly mistakes.

3

REVIEW OF PROCESSES, PROCEDURES, AND STANDARDS

THE PPS SOLUTION

*O*h PPS, how most people hate you for no good reason! Processes, Procedures, and Standards. These are the money-makers of the big 6, er big 4, er, big 2 Business Consulting Firms. The Showtime show House of Lies takes the idea that business consultants are just snake oil salesmen full of hot air to the next level. I love that show because they do manage to use some of the right buzzwords I've heard (and used) in the last 25 years. But like any other show, it's more "dramedy" than reality when it comes to fixing companies.

In my experience, most senior executives in large companies ($100+ million) think their departments use PPS. When interviewing department heads in the same companies, that percentage drops significantly to about 25%. When interviewing staff in the same departments, virtually no one would call whatever written documentation they had as being usable processes, procedures or standards! Everyone explained that these documents were old, obsolete, or otherwise not applicable and that the company has changed enough things to make them useless.

Naturally, there are exceptions. Companies that have become certified in standards, such as ISO 9001 or even ISO 27001 must have PPS to become certified, and so they absolutely have PPS - for the areas covered by requirements. For that matter they have PPS on how to keep their PPS up to date. Of course, companies that practice Kaizen, or have Six Sigma programs, or that have contracts that require PPS, try to have it to whatever degree they need to.

But let's look at the typical small to mid-sized business. Selling $25 million top line and maybe getting $2 million in bottom line profit. How many of them have up to date, meaning actually usable, PPS? Not many at all and if you're like the average company in the US, you probably don't either.

So what's so great about Standards or Processes anyway? Well, to put it into money terms, they allow you to have a more standardized product or service delivery for a lower cost. So you can do stuff cheaper, and of consistent quality. With business, unlike art, variety is the enemy of success. No matter how much people like your product, if you can't repeat what you did, you will never taste the reward of that success. Repeatability allows you to make and test incremental changes. Quantifying the results of those incremental improvements is impossible without consistency.

Standards define what things are, what they need to be produced, and what to measure the final product against. Procedures describe how things are made or assembled, or designed in a repeatable way. These are step by step guides like Ikea furniture might include. Processes are the big picture view of the business operations. They discuss standards and procedures and show processes necessary to drive the business.

If so many businesses operate without them, then why would small businesses need them? Well, competition favors those who can offer the best thing at the most reasonable price. Notice I didn't say cheapest since you have to compare apples to apples, not oranges!

There are many advantages to standardization and continual improvement. I had the pleasure of having the W. Edwards Deming Institute as a client many years ago. Deming is the American responsible for most of the Japanese auto industry overtaking US automakers in such a short time. Today Toyota is the world's largest automobile company. I happily defer to the Institute for training on the benefits of the Deming method or to a plethora of Six Sigma training programs for quality and process improvement.

Most of the Fortune 500 companies utilize some form of PPS, and for one I am happy to name a company where I consulted. P&G - Procter, and Gamble - is leaps and bounds ahead of any other company I have worked with in their adherence to PPS and continuous improvement. While I came into P&G with multiple certifications in various technology and business practices, I was very happily surprised at the level of process control and improvement at every level of the company with which I interacted. As you can imagine it is much harder to ensure processes are followed and monitored in a large company than a small one - there are just so many more moving pieces - but P&G managed to lead the way for other large businesses. It is interesting to note that in 2017 P&G cut $140 million in advertising online. There may be many factors that played into that decision, but a significant factor was the lack of tangible return on investment. Unlike companies that act like lemmings, following one another blindly, P&G evaluates all their contracts and expenses to be sure they are performing at the level of expectations. This process is very uncommon in small business and almost unheard of in large corporate America. P&G determined that traditional media like television, print, and radio had a better quantifiable return on their branding spend. After all, it's impossible to have an ad-blocker block out commercials from the radio station you are listening to in the car - and that includes SiriusXM!

4

HUMAN RESOURCES OPTIMIZATION

ARE THE RIGHT PEOPLE IN THE RIGHT POSITIONS?

*I*n Chapter 2 I talked about hiring well. In this chapter we continue looking at employees. One area that I've seen neglected in all but the largest companies is that of re-evaluating employees and moving them around to the most efficient utilization within the organization. So how does a company go about doing that?.

I talk frequently about the evolution of employees both from a business need, and from an employee perspective. An early-stage startup business needs flexible people who are jacks-of-all-trades and masters of none. The need to 'jump in and help' is much greater in an early startup than a billion dollar corporation. That ability to jump in and help becomes a liability as the company grows large enough to have managers and specialists. Specialization in departments is the key to growing a business from $10 million to $100 million and beyond. So does that mean that most businesses start replacing their founding employees as soon as they reach $10 million? To the contrary, most businesses simply promote their generalists, jacks-of-all-trades to senior management positions as the company grows. Do these people grow with the company needs, specialize in some department and become experts? Sometimes, but mostly not.

Many large companies are filled with managers who know less about their departments than both their boss and their employees. These generalists are quick to offer to help and jump in - that is why they were hired in the first place, remember? But this ability is rarely a good thing as a manager. They are loved by their employees because they act just like one of the guys, always covering for their team and throwing themselves on any failures, knowing that their long service to the company and their ability in the early years to do what was needed will ensure that their departmental failures are overlooked. This behavior is not good for the business.

So am I saying that an HR optimization is simply the elimination of all tenured employees from a company? No, of course not. Some employees do indeed find a specialization and end up focusing on it as the company itself grows. These people represent truly the only group of employees that it pays to hang on to for extended periods of time. They grew with the company, grew into specialists, and yet hold a lot of wisdom - knowledge and experience about failures in the early days. These are the employees that have been with Apple and Microsoft for 25+ years. The people at Google and Amazon that have been there over 15 years. There are very few of them, and they have shown an upward progress within the companies, not simply because of tenure, but rather because they have changed as the needs of the company have changed.

So the real question is how do you separate the people who have changed with the needs of the company from the people who have merely hung-on? After all, the latter group may very well be more liked by their staff, and their willingness to always say "yes" to helping others is seen as an asset. It is very challenging for most business owners, and even non-owner executives, to admit that these employees are replaceable.

However, for the betterment of the company, the trees need to be pruned on a regular basis. The only way that I've experienced this happening is with having an outsider come in to observe and evaluate management. Generally this will be a management consultant or some similar outsider. Their job is to figure out if the people in the roles within the organization are the ideal people who would be hired if that position were open today, or if they are simply filling that role by default, or as a reward for being with the company a long time, or perhaps for being the only person who didn't take a step back when the role needed to be filled during a busy growth phase in the past. A business consultant will be able to figure out who is accelerating the growth of the company, and who is slowing it down.

The one exception that I've experienced was in a Fortune 500 company years ago. I had been closely working with a senior employee who had been with the company for nearly 20 years. One of my jobs was to evaluate his performance and report back to management. As I got to know this person I started to recognize him for a very dedicated employee who had a bit too much generalist in him. I didn't think he would be climbing the management ladder but felt that he would be a great asset to any quick response team in the company - essentially a "jump into the fire" team inside the organization.

I was surprised when I found out he had in fact years earlier been promoted to a large department manager. I was wondering if he had failed at that to be demoted back to a senior non-management employee. As it turned out he had not! He realized after a few years that he hated running a team of 40 people. He much preferred to be the guy in the trenches that others can turn to for help, rather than planning staff reviews and working with project managers and business analysts. He actually saw his own strengths and weaknesses and made the proactive decision to leave management. This was a big benefit to the company because he was able to do what he was good at, rather than be a shitty manager.

Unfortunately, after I was done with that client, I found out they had laid him off anyway. I didn't hesitate one moment and recommended him to be brought onto a project I was now running for another Fortune 500 company. This new team needed precisely this kind of experience and energy. He was much more valuable as the lead triage guy than as a director or group manager. Of course his experience level would pay at the level of a director!

This was not the only instance I've found someone a position after they were let go from a company I was consulting. If you read my earlier book I'm sure you will remember a few of those stories.

5

POST-HIRE INTERVIEWS

WHY DO THEM?

*M*ost people have never heard of post-hire interviews, but companies that want to maximize their employee motivation unquestionably need to conduct these interviews on a regular basis. What is a post-hire interview? Well, you may be tempted to think it's just another name for an annual Human Resources (HR) review, but it is not. Let's be honest, most companies don't do reviews unless an employee asks, and the ones that do, generally do it as a checkbox only to let an employee know how much of a raise or bonus they should expect. Post-hire interviews are quite similar to the type of conversation the employee went through when they were interviewing for their current role.

I'm trying to save you money - so here is what I said relating to HR management in my last book.

Promote people based on the needs of the company and the quality of the work.

> *Give raises based on changes in competitive wage*
> *landscape to retain good employees.*
> *Give one-time bonuses to reward exceptional*
> *performance.*

If we break that down, it becomes clear that to know who to promote and how to analyze the quality of someone's work, you need to have a clear picture of what that person has done, is doing, and is most interested in doing moving forward. There is no better person to answer those questions than the employee. Sure, you can look at departmental successes and failures or get an assessment of that employee from their manager, but that may not truly reflect all their efforts and certainly does not include their future interests.

It is useful to have the employee summarize their activities before an interview. While some people dread writing work summaries, I believe this is one of the most valuable tools for everyone involved. If an employee can summarize their wins in their current role, much in the way they would do on LinkedIn or their resume, then you will have a much better idea of what they see as their primary wins. This may show that their priorities and interests were different than what their manager would think. Listening to employees describe their daily responsibilities, successes, and failures in their own words is one of the simplest, but least utilized techniques to evaluate past performance and even more importantly future potential. I can't count the number of times I saw a huge disconnect between what employees thought their priorities were, and what management assumed they were. Similarly having an employee describe their focus and passion for future projects can be a telltale of future success or failure of their next project they are assigned to.

Treating this conversation as a post-hire interview sets the stage for the employee to be in the same "selling themselves to the company" mentality they had when they initially got hired. While I don't think the stress of continually losing your job is good for anyone, I do believe it is beneficial to get people used to re-selling themselves to the company every year. It forces employees to know what their wins and strengths are and motivates them to do more than the bare minimum work necessary to stay employed, which unfortunately many people use as their target. It is also useful for the employee because they get a regular opportunity to toot their own horn without more aggressive employees or management getting in the way. Of course, if the employee should become a poor fit for the business, this process better prepares them for a job search. This may be of minor concern to you as the owner, but remember, you are interviewing people and trying to find the best ones to fill your open roles. You would not want to pass up a more qualified person just because they do not do a good job representing their past accomplishments, would you?

For the company, there is one additional benefit. Since the goal of any company is to find and the most qualified resources for the tasks the business needs to be done, HR should always be looking for new candidates, even when there is no specific open role. The best way to compare existing employees to potential candidates is by having existing employees go through the same type of process, namely an interview, as the candidates. This allows for a better apples to apples comparison.

The core of my message is that people should be listened to and not simply have their work product evaluated. Understanding the why and how can only be achieved when they describe their own actions.

As part of my consulting process with a new company, I always conduct these interviews and ask employees to create a job description based on what they actually do, not what they were hired to do. What I can say after years of doing this, is that employees do much, much more than their managers think they do. They also generally set their priorities for tasks based on reactive factors. People in all areas of a company will usually try to do the 'big picture' role that they were hired to do about 20% of the time while spending 80% of the time dealing with problems that arise on a daily basis. For that matter, often even consuming large amounts of their day in helping other employees with their tasks. The overwhelming majority of the time, executives and management are not aware of these activities and frequently see the employee as not being very productive.

There is another benefit that can come out of an in-depth post-hire interview, namely that an employee seems busy to everyone, but is, in fact, horrible at managing time. They may appear to be very busy and in fact, work longer hours than others, but upon examination of all their activities, it becomes evident that they merely accomplish tasks at a slower pace than everyone assumes. This is a situation that I had experienced with a client several years ago. There was a concern that Information Technology (IT) related problems were holding back the business. While looking at the IT projects two things became clear to me. First was that we had a classic "Bob" problem - which I describe in detail in my last book. Essentially a Bob is a person who does their job without any repeatable processes and becomes the keeper of all knowledge about a particular department in the business and often becoming quite defensive about institutional knowledge as well.

Second, the employee in question was very inefficient in how they conducted their activities at work. For example, someone who justifies their poor decisions by saving some small amount of money for the company, but to achieve those savings, they will need to spend hundreds of hours of time - which is worth much more than the savings realized - figuring out how to implement the solution. This hurts the company in multiple ways. It prevents this employee from working on other tasks required by the business, and it creates systems that are officially unsupported and can only be used by the person who created them in the first place.

If the answer to the question "How does that work?" is the name of a person rather than a process, your business has "Bob" problems.

6

BENEFITS PACKAGE EVALUATION

HOW ATTRACTIVE ARE WE?

*T*he benefits that most businesses offer today are vastly different than what was the norm 20 years ago. Of course, the expectations of employees are also different today. Benefits include both tangible and intangible items that the employee receives in trade for their labor. The most significant component is undoubtedly salary. Although we have seen a de-emphasis on just salary with Millennials, for the company it still represents the single biggest cost of the employee total package. That benefit is relatively easy to evaluate and adjust based on location and similarity to positions you have filled. I would like to think that most companies do a decent job of checking their competition to determine the appropriate salary, but just in case you don't, here is a quick guide.

When it becomes evident that a new role has to be created to expand the company or that a position needs to be filled because it has become vacant, the first step should be to re-evaluate all the requirements for the role. Once the position is clearly defined, the next step is to start searching job websites for similar positions. This may help you add or remove components based on what other businesses advertise, and it should give you a good idea of what the market demand and pay rates are for such a position. Remember, the amount that a company is willing to pay for a specific role should depend predominantly on market conditions, as long as the company can bear the cost that the market demands. If the company cannot afford to be competitive, it may be necessary to reduce the requirements of the role until the company can compete for talent. There is no reason to pay above market rates to fill any position unless there is a time crunch, and in that case, you should still pay market rates, and offer a hiring cash bonus tied to a minimum time on the job.

If you think that you can get a better person by offering more money for a particular role, you are mistaken. That is the "common wisdom" which I find to be empirically incorrect. Let's think about it for a moment. Suppose you are looking for a Director of Finance and the market rate is $95k + benefits for that role. You can pay $115k based on your budgeting. Could you find a person for $115k for that role? Of course, and they will be happy to tell you why they are worth the extra money. However, if you do further research, you might find that in your area you can hire a CFO for $120k. Of course, a $120k CFO may not be at the top of the chart, but a qualified mid-level CFO candidate should be able to come in with much more knowledge and, most importantly, more experience than an above average cost Director-level candidate.

Now if you don't have a CFO and you are hiring a

Director of Finance, would you be better off with someone at a middle stage of their career or would you be better off hiring someone at a later stage of their career with more experience for just $5k more? If you already have a CFO, naturally part of his job should be making sure that the company does not spend any more money than it needs to on any position in the business!

Like any rule, there are exceptions. If you have extenuating circumstances which justify paying above market, like a time crunch or needing someone who is more self-guided because there is no immediate supervisor for that role, it is entirely ok to pay more, but with a caveat. You have to recognize that you are addressing a problem in another part of the business with a less than ideal solution. If there is a time crunch, the company should have started looking sooner. If there is lack of immediate supervision, maybe that is the role that needs to be filled first or management functions consolidated. The bottom line is that you should never need to pay more than the market demand for a person to fill a particular role with a specific set of requirements.

Hiring someone who is overqualified for a role is okay as long as you are not overpaying that overqualified person. Hiring someone with no more qualifications for more money is a poor business decision, and hiring someone with fewer qualifications is always a bad idea. Notice I say qualifications and not just experience. The minimal qualifications should have been determined for the role and should include experience, knowledge, and other elements which qualify someone for that role in the company.

So what about the other components of benefits beyond

salary? The second largest cost to business for benefits after salary is either medical insurance if the company provides a substantial portion on behalf of the employee, or vacation pay if the company has a generous vacation policy. Other costs these days include company provided food/beverages, activity reimbursements for things like health club memberships, company clothing or even car expenses, bonus or profit sharing, office furnishings (especially standing desks and Aeron chairs), and in some companies, games or relaxation are an employee expense.

While corporations like Google are famous for having free catered meals, massages, pool tables and other games for their employees, this trend is now making way to smaller companies. The appearance of a coffee shop, with soft music playing while baristas serve espresso drinks made with expensive Italian coffee machines, is becoming a more common sight in businesses. In my opinion, this is partly driven by actual desires of the younger workforce and partly by management assumptions that these are the kinds of benefits that attract young workers.

Benefits of a 'cool' work environment and free food at the office are examples of Consumptive Benefits. These benefits attract people who want to make work feel more like home. Often the positive result is longer working hours for employees who have no reason to go home or to a coffee shop as the work environment is equally as comfortable for them.

Benefits such as longer vacation pay or 401k matching programs are Sustaining Benefits as they do not provide an immediate benefit to the employee and are appreciated by employees who value personal time and individual investment planning. These employees will have the same attitude toward long-term company investments and will champion long-term goals and solutions that may not achieve a result for an extended duration of time.

I do not put a value judgment on one type of employee vs. the other. They both have pros and cons for the company, but as long as the benefits selection that the company provides is chosen with these results in mind, they should help attract and keep a particular type of employee personality. However do keep in mind that if a business invests significantly in "cool" work environment but only 50% of employees value that, then that investment is wasted on the other 50% of employees, unnecessarily increasing the effective cost of the per employee benefits.

Interestingly, both types of employees like the remote working or work-anywhere option. The former like the ability to work from a coffee shop near their house or to meet at a remote-workspace with their colleagues once a week. The latter like being able to save money on commuting to the office and have the ability to work from the house. Remote working is a topic that could be its own chapter or even a full book. Let me just say I am a firm believer that almost any job which does not require physical access to specialized company equipment can be done as well, or better, remotely. The biggest impediment I have observed to having a remote workforce is the lack

I have seen the shift from cube farms to open offices and now am seeing the swing back. A large Fortune 500 company that I consulted with years ago had a rather efficiently designed scheme. It crammed as many employees into cubicles near windows as it could, while using the inner space in the building for lots of small conference rooms. The idea was that people are sitting near windows, but if two or more people need to meet in private, they just grab a conference room as needed.

This sounds good in principle, and I'm sure some business efficiency consulting firm got paid plenty to suggest this arrangement, however in practice this didn't work well at all. People who were naturally extroverted tended to spend a lot of time in conversations with others around them in this very tight seating arrangement. While people who work best in quiet surroundings and with little distraction either struggled with noise-blocking headphones. Others gave up and simply created dummy meetings to be able to sit in a windowless room and get their work done. This meant that conference rooms were rarely available, while the overall productivity of the office was reduced due to unrelenting chatter.

While people today think that cube farms are horrible, it's important to remember than cubes were actually a solution to the problems of an open office in the 1950s. As white collar jobs increased, companies found themselves with more and more employees who worked behind a desk rather than operating a machine. Initially, these desks were needed to hold paper for reading and writing. Back then most things were handwritten, to be given to a typing pool to reproduce as typed text. Businesses simply borrowed the solution to this growing need from someplace it had already been used - in schools. The same arrangement of desks into rows, albeit with nicer and larger desks, was utilized. Keep in mind that back then most people didn't even have telephones on their desks unless they were part of a sales team. So you had a bunch of employees sitting at desks and quietly reading and writing. They would generally have an IN and OUT boxes on their desks to be filled or collected by roving bands of clerks. Management had offices on the outside perimeter surrounding the desks and would meet in their managers' offices to discuss what they were working on.

As technology progressed, telephones became a more common fixture on desks and by the 80's, computers found their way into the workforce occupying even more desk space. Putting up noise absorbent cube walls around the desks allowed companies to provide some level of noise reduction, increasing the storage space in cubes by going vertical and increasing the concentration of employees in a given size space. By putting storage over the desk, cubes could be made to be 44in wide and replaced typical 60in desks. That allowed companies to add more meeting rooms while reducing the size of management offices. This way people who worked in cubes could have a meeting place even when it didn't involve a manager.

The modern open office, as I recently experienced at a client, has massive long desks like those in an Apple store or a coffee shop which accommodate up to 12 people per desk. There is no privacy and no noise protection, so virtually everyone has headphones on to block out external noise. While the desk space per person is abysmal in this open office, it is augmented by soft loungers, coffee tables, and hanging chairs that one might find on a porch. People move throughout the day from location to location - seemingly trying to find a level of privacy or comfort that an open office does a great job of preventing.

As odd as it seems to me, having an open office plan is still perceived as a desirable benefit by many younger workers. I guess I'm old school. Give me an office or let me work from home! Either way, I want quiet and uninterrupted work space! My advice is don't just dive into the open office trend - figure out what works for your workflow first, then your individual employee preferences second - and only if possible, adopt a policy of flexible office space that doesn't break the bank or result in one employee getting much more expensive furniture than another.

7

FINANCIAL REVIEW

HOW HEALTHY ARE WE?

*M*ost business owners and CEOs I work with have a very good idea of the top line sales numbers for their companies. Generally, that is a number they get from the CFO or in a sales report. However, the number who know their current and trending bottom line profit is drastically smaller. While that number will have the most significant effect on their yearly compensation, it is a much smaller and less impressive number, and so the top line sales number is how most companies compare themselves to others. Not by how profitable they are, but rather by how much they collected in gross sales. Of course, it is important to keep that number growing, but not at the expense of all other financial considerations.

Sales are great! But sales that cost as much money to generate as they bring in are vastly different from sales that have a healthy margin resulting in a higher net profit. So when comparing sales from one company to another, keep in mind you are most likely comparing apples to pears if not oranges. If we dig deeper into financials, most CEOs happily shrug off any expectation of knowledge about the state of finance to the CFO. They assume the CFO is managing things well and that he will advise the CEO of any hiccups. I see this "what me worry?" attitude quite often. The reality is, all employees - including executives - have an incentive to minimize the appearance of problems and maximize positive appearance. It's human nature to do that. However a diligent CEO, and for that matter, any thorough manager will review and understand financials for the company or at least their department on a regular basis. The job of the CFO is to answer the WHY questions relating to financial health. Their job is not to magically ensure financial health.

How can I say that is not their job? Isn't that exactly their job? Well, let me explain the "unconventional" perspective here. The executive tasked with ensuring money is coming into the company is usually the VP of Sales, or the recent en vogue title, Chief Revenue Officer. They focus on increasing sales. That is the number by which they will be judged. Marketing may or may not be a separate department from Sales, but either way, their job is to increase the lead flow for Sales, so they are judged predominantly on lead generation. Production Management or Service Management is responsible for providing the things or services at the least cost to the company, that Sales sells to the customer. Customer Service is responsible for maximizing customer satisfaction by converting unhappy customers to happy repeat customers and ensuring happy customers stay happy. HR is responsible for finding the best employees at the best prices and keeping them from leaving, as long as they are performing well. The COO is responsible for the smooth and efficient operation of all production/delivery departments. So every one of these departments has a more significant impact than the CFO on the amount of money coming in as well as the amount of money spent by the company. Indeed the CFO does not decide how much money comes in, how fast it comes in, how much is spent, or how quickly. Certainly, they have an opinion about these things and can sometimes pull the emergency brake, but ultimately the office of the CFO is there to be sure that invoices are sent out, bills get paid, and the company does not miss payroll. The CEO needs to use the recommendations of the CFO to align the company vision with the costs that all the departments incur realizing that vision. The CFO comes up with strategies and suggestions to finance these activities. Leaving the decision on marketing spend or product acquisition costs solely up to the CFO would just as quickly bankrupt a company as ignoring the advice of the CFO.

My primary recommendation for CEOs and all other department heads is to become familiar with central accounting documents of your business or department. Learn to read the P&L, Balance Sheet, and Cashflow Statement and do so on a monthly basis. Understand the cost of operations, cost of goods, and cost of sales. Be sure you can understand financial decisions and their impact on the company today, as well as in the future. Spending money today to achieve better sales tomorrow may be a great idea or a horrible one depending on where your company is and where it is going.

With the small exception of well-funded silicon valley

unicorns, businesses exist to generate profit. Even Not-For-Profit businesses need to generate a profit; they just use that profit to further a cause - a different mission statement - rather than passing it on to stockholders. Become more familiar with the drivers in your company that can affect profitability and don't leave it to the CFO to tell you when there is bad news.

I had a client that was losing money even though they had very healthy sales. Their expenses were eating away all profit, and in fact, the business was projected to run out of cash reserves if something didn't change. When I came in, my first action was reviewing the financial documents. My second action was to fire the CFO. Having done that, I chastised the CEO for not paying better attention to the economic state of the business. I explained to him that hiring a CFO does not mean he can ignore everything related to financial health of the company. In the course of my tenure at that client, I was able to not only stop the financial bleeding but reverse the trend toward profitability. In fact, while sales were down 18% one year, I was able to increase net profits 220% in the same period by putting in more stringent controls on spending.

But it's not all good news, as a year later I ended up hiring a new CFO for the company and unfortunately, I trusted the CFO too much. I took him at his word on the financial state of things and eventually found out he had been neglecting his job and resulting in a mess of accounts that had to get sorted out. Had I heeded my own advice back then, I would have been able to catch the problem sooner. Of course, that is the benefit of hindsight.

Learn from your own mistakes, but better yet, learn from the mistakes of others. This is the wisdom of past mistakes I mentioned when talking about hiring seasoned employees.

8

SYSTEMATIZED PROJECT MANAGEMENT

MORE PRODUCTIVITY, FEWER PROBLEMS

I have already talked about the benefits of Standards, Processes, and Procedures, but all those become irrelevant if they are not followed or kept up to date with changes. The focus of project management is to do just that. Maybe more accurately, project management utilizes those tools to ensure highest efficiency and resiliency for the operations of the business.

Whether the business creates products, buys them to resell, or provide a service, project management is there to help manage the parts that make up the whole. Project Management, as a discreet corporate discipline, has been around for a few decades now. At least 4500 years in fact as the earliest examples of Project Management can be found in hieroglyphs from the building of the Great Pyramid of Giza. More recently, about 100 years ago, the Gantt chart was developed as a standard visual method for tracking task progress, milestones and dependencies within a project. Along the way Critical path and Work Breakdown Structures were coined and became part of modern Project Management. In 1969, the Project Management Institute was formed and to this day creates a curriculum and certifies people as Certified Project Managers. Decades ago I went through this training process and I still send employees of companies I consult for to get their training from PMI because even if certification is not needed, their training provides a baseline education that every good project manager should have.

The best way to describe the benefits of using a project management system is that it is another tool in the CEO and management arsenal to ensure better efficiency and productivity while minimizing the impact of problems along the way. If you were to look back on a past situation where issues arose which affected your ability to deliver to your customers or a problem that affected your business internally, looking back with 20/20 hindsight you are probably able to analyze what happened and how it could have been prevented. Now, imagine being able to see that problem before it had any time to make an impact. Imagine having contingency plans already in place before the problem even arose. Imagine being able to easily prevent the problem from affecting your ability to deliver to the client. That is the ultimate goal and benefit of project management. Greater insight into the process; faster identification when problems arise; and pre-planned avoidance and resolution tactics to minimize impact. In a nutshell, the discipline of project management is all about making obstacles have less impact on your ability to deliver results.

For the last eight years, for every company I have come in to consult, I have started or updated a project management system and sent at least one employee to take the PMI certification classes. Keep in mind that a project management system is not just software. It is also the directions for how people will use project management in the company including procedures for the PM. While certification is not required, having the same understanding of the terminology that all certified project managers use, as well as the rationale for the proper way to set up critical paths for projects, is well worth the price of PMI classes.

One other thing I want to make clear for those new to using project management. A project manager is different than a group manager. The PM is not responsible for HR responsibilities for the group such as performance and reviews. They are also not responsible for the department budgets the way a group manager is. The PM is responsible for monitoring and managing progress of projects which may include people from multiple groups.

9

OFFICE SPACE SEARCHES

OPTIMIZING OFFICE FOR CULTURE

I've already mentioned open offices and relaxation facilities in a previous chapter. So let me briefly reiterate my position is that the best space for a person to do work in, is the space where they are most productive. While that statement may seem obvious, quite often the decision on who works where is based on the availability of space and preference of management. If someone is like me and works best in a quiet, uninterrupted environment, then they can work either from home or work in an office with a closed door at the company location. I do not work nearly as efficiently at a coffee shop with ambient music or noise, nor an open office which very much resembles a coffee shop. A cubicle is a middle ground, as long as the ambient noise if held low. For someone who works better in a coffee shop type environment, it may be that their home or an open office would also work well. The bottom line is not to assume that all employees will be most effective and efficient in a single environment that an executive happens to like.

For that reason among others, I've always been a big fan of allowing - and even encouraging - employees to work from home and avoid coming into the office other than for specific meetings. Want another another reason to encourage people to work from home? Harvard Business Review wrote an article titled "To Raise Productivity, Let More Employees Work from Home" which I think you can still find online which supports what I've noticed empirically over the last 20 years. People who work from home work more efficiently. According to that article people working from home not only had higher satisfaction rates than their office counterparts, but they had a 13.5% higher productivity. Another huge benefit to hiring workers to work from home is removing geographic limitations. You can hire the most qualified people even if they do not live in the city the company has an office.

So, what have I recommended for office space? While changing offices is not necessarily a common theme in my past consulting, I have been involved with commercial realtors for many companies I have worked with. I've opened new regional offices for companies, consolidated facilities from different states, and planned whole office relocations. What I have found over the last 20 years are two main points. First, the variety of commercial real estate has vastly more range of choices than residential real estate. Meaning that if an office might work for you, but isn't perfect, keep looking because there is probably one which is much closer to perfection just around the corner. Secondly, commercial realtors are even less interested in showing you more than five properties than residential realtors. Sure, it makes sense that someone working on a commission of two months rent would love nothing more than to have you take one of the offices they show you on the first day. They make the same amount, and total time at that point was less than 8 hours for them. The more time they spend with you, the less they make per hour.

But since you will be in your office for 3-7 years, depending on the lease, it's important to take the time to find the perfect location because that decision will affect everyone in the company who doesn't work remotely. Taking time and focusing on what the client wants in an office has allowed me to find Class A rated office space for Class B rated pricing. I've done this many times by subleasing prime office space from companies who have shrunk or moved and no longer need the space. By spending the time and getting the agent to understand you won't sign until you are ready, you can invest the time to find a location which ideally addresses your needs for the coming years.

Everyone has different preferences, but what I found is that there are three common uses of office space. Those are: house your employees, provide a location with a good environment for meetings, and produce your product. The latter may be a warehouse location, or it may be a table, but generally, every company has those needs to varying degrees. When it comes to meetings, there are certain things which help foster a productive outcome. Whiteboards for brainstorming have been very common for decades and a good meeting room will have at least one wall that has a full-width whiteboard. In some startup office situations, I've recommended using 4x8 sheets of plastic bath board sold at Home Depot for use in waterproofing bathrooms. Those sheets work perfectly for writing and erasing dry erase markers. Naturally, for more established companies there are some better-looking options. Aside from a whiteboard, a good meeting room should have the ability to project a computer, either onto the same whiteboard using a projector or to a large screen TV. Lastly, the thing that most people forget is that the room needs to set the right tone for a meeting.

Our environment affects not just our moods, but also how we view the world. This is why it is so common to see meeting rooms in highrise office buildings with floor to ceiling glass. The birds-eye-view of the city stimulates big picture thinking and helps people imagine in ways they would not if merely sitting in a cube on a Skype call. Another example of altering the mood in a conference room is the use of large aquariums. Years ago I had set up a conference room in my company which didn't have any windows with a whiteboard and projector, as well as a 12 person table. The room was just not very appealing though, and people wanted to leave as soon as a meeting was over. I ended up installing three large aquarium tanks to fill an entire wall on one side of the room. Having the tropical fish swimming around, moving rocks, chasing snails and doing other fish things completely changed the atmosphere of the place. People were much less anxious to leave and there was more casual conversation in the room. I actually had clients and vendors both mention that the fish made them feel very relaxed. Of course, this is not a surprise to anyone who knows Asian cultural perspective on fish ponds. Before there were ever glass aquariums, there were koi ponds with exotic and unique breeds of carp creating a relaxing atmosphere. Think about the many Asian restaurants with a tradition of using aquariums to encourage a peaceful and relaxed atmosphere. But also keep in mind that a dirty aquarium is very unappealing, so figure in the cost of ongoing maintenance if you go that route.

10

SUCCESSION PLANNING

HOW TO LEAVE ON YOUR TERMS

*M*uch like parents hope their children will have happy lives when they leave the nest, most business founders hope their business will be able to survive them. Not necessarily survive their death, but rather survive diminished involvement. I will cover different exit strategies from a company in the next chapter, but right now let's look at one that may require the most time, namely succession planning.

While often this is simply a replacement of the founder or CEO upon retirement, there are smaller, partial successions that need to take place over the lifetime of the business. Most companies in the US with revenues over $500,000 are founded by two people who have slightly different skill sets but who have to be able to do everything the business requires. If they are successful and the company grows, then they can hire employees to take on some of the tasks they have been doing themselves. So in a sense succession planning should continuously be happening in a growing business. As the business grows, less functions should be done by any one person, with new employees being hired to specialize.

Where this gets tricky is usually when there are ten employees in the business. By that time all of the repetitive, menial, tedious, and simple tasks have been handed over to someone else. As the company continues to grow, the complexity of work that needs to be done by the founder keeps increasing.

So how do you, as the business owner, get to the point of needing to hire a COO or even a CEO to run the company? Shouldn't that be your job as the founder? How can you trust someone who didn't start the business to keep growing it and making it more successful? If you can answer those questions, you are well on your way to having a succession plan. If not, keep reading.

I want to emphasize a clear distinction between leadership roles within the company. For example the executive officer and ownership overlap when the founder run the business, but they do not at all have to be the same people. As a founder CEO of a business, you work hard to increase its value. The salary you pay yourself is in "compensation for work of the CEO" which you are doing on behalf of the company. Any dividends or profit disbursement you pay yourself are the partial compensation for your ownership in the business. When you sell the business, you receive the bulk portion of your "compensation for ownership."

So let me ask this question: If you had someone else do the administrating work of the business, while you work on creating new products or services, could that be a better use of your time to increase the value of the company? Keep in mind that the person hired as the CEO should be someone who is excellent at the administrative running of the business to ensure fewer operational mistakes and therefore faster growth. The result would be a company run by someone whose skill set is focused on the operations of the business, allowing you, as the founder, to focus on where your skills have the greatest impact. If your skillset happens to be the same as what is needed for a CEO, then it's a perfect fit. But I've met very few founders who make good CEOs. They are too creative, too interested in marketing, or very good at product development to be only focused on the CEO role.

Conversely, if the above scenario sounds horrible to you and you would never let anyone run your company as long as you were alive then you probably have a lifestyle business. Now I'm not trying to insult you, but instead make the distinction between businesses which predominantly exist to provide a great lifestyle to the owner and businesses which are focused on increasing their value for an eventual sale. Quite often the difference between the two is whether the company has partners or has investors (Angels, VCs, Institutional Investors). Investors have no interest in running the company and do not get a salary and dividends are usually small, so they look for an eventual opportunity to earn back their investment.

So what is wrong with running and growing my own business? Why would I need to hire someone else to do it when I'm the one who has successfully grown it this far? Those sound like reasonable questions, so let me explain the benefits of moving to a role you have the best skills for in your business, with time. I spend quite a bit of time in my previous book talking about the changing needs of a growing business. This change happens at all levels. The jacks-of-all-trades employees you needed to succeed when the company was a startup, will hold you back as it grows. The need for you as the founder to be involved in every interaction in the business which was so vital to keeping your clients happy at the beginning is a detriment to growth at a later stage of business.

In my last book on this topic, I said "You're now running a different type of organization. You're now the conductor of an orchestra, rather than the first violin." To use this analogy, the business starts as a solo, grows to a duet, then a quartet, a chamber orchestra and finally a full orchestra.

The skills which got you to where you are today are not the skills you need to get to the next level. So adapt with the business in leadership, learning new skills, letting go of the need to be as connected with the day-to-day inner workings of the company, allowing people to make mistakes which you would not have made yourself. Or find someone who can do that for you while you remaining the owner but focus your sights on some non-operational aspect of growing the company. Many founders have taken on roles as Chief Scientist, Chief Researcher, Chief Marketing Officer, or Chief Disruptasaurus - yes that last one is a real title from a past client! Letting someone run your company starts to feel much better when the value of your company goes up faster!

But if your passion is operational leadership in a changing organization - then congratulations, you are one of a very small group of people who can adapt at the pace required to not just run a company, but to keep growing a business from its humble startup beginnings to a billion dollar company. If you choose to stay in the leadership role, your success or failure will be very evident by the growth of the company. Continual growth year over year is a good bet that you are able to modify your skills to provide the leadership the business needs. On the other hand stagnation in sales, drop in bottom line profit, a loss of market share all point to a lack of the type of leadership the company ultimately needed. You as a founder will always be an owner until you sell the business, but you do not have to be the person who is running the company day to day. In fact as the owner, or the chair of the board of directors, you have the power to hire and fire the CEO. So if that job is not best suited to you. Hire someone for whom it's a perfect fit.

I guess what I'd really like you to remember about this chapter is that the operational leadership needs of the company go through a substantial change between a startup and a $250 million business. It is entirely okay to hire leadership at different times within that range rather than having to hold the burden of leadership for the entire duration.

Just remember you can always replace a CEO as the owner, but it's much harder to replace yourself even if you should.

11

EXIT STRATEGY

WHEN TO SELL

*A*s the previous chapter focused on the changing needs of the company and the changing role of the CEO, in this section, I want to focus specifically on what it means to leave the company you started and grew.

The two most common reasons for exiting a business are the sale of the company or retirement. Hopefully, if it is retirement, there is also a sale of some type, even if to relatives! In planning an exit strategy, it is essential to have a realistic goal that is backed up by sound justifications. Secondarily, it is vital to put the best face on the business before starting the sale or transition process. Lastly, emotional ties to the company need to be substantially limited or cut altogether. At this stage, your measure of success should be the value you can obtain from the business, not how it survives without you. Remember, you paid yourself a salary for the job you did day to day. Selling the company is your payment for originally investing it in and having owned it all these years.

If your goal for the business from day one was to sell it, not merely to have a business that supports your lifestyle, then the prep work for selling it should be pretty straightforward. You should have at least three years of clean, audited financial statements. You should have shown growth or profit for the last 3-5 years. You should have processes and procedures in place so that the business can operate with minimal disruption even if a key employee leaves. And you should have done your research about the valuation of comparable businesses.

Having managed a business sale for one of my clients, I can say that even seemingly well-organized businesses struggle to go through the due diligence process that is required by buyers. So the sooner you are ready, the faster the sales process will happen and the smoother it will go. For instance, having your finances audited is expensive and time-consuming, so most privately held businesses do it only occasionally or if required to do so. Having three years of audited books will minimize questions relating to finances for the buyer. After all the buyer is trying to learn as much as possible about both the pros and cons of your business in just a matter of months and with millions of dollars at stake they want to have a complete picture!

While buyers will look at business sales to get an idea of how well the products sell and estimate what the market potential is with the changes they will introduce, bottom line profits will nonetheless have a significant impact on the size of the offer. In fact, the size of the initial payment for the sale will be most affected by the profit potential of the business. If the offer is a 30/25/25/20 deal over three years, the first number is almost never going to be higher than the profit potential of the company in one year. Most business sale offers are based on a multiple of EBITDA - Earnings Before Interest, Tax, Depreciation, and Amortization - and not on sales volume per year.

While EBITDA is not the best measure to grow your business, it is a really common measure when it comes to selling businesses. If you plan on selling your business, you should start looking at your EBITDA several years before the planned sale and decide if decisions today will affect the EBITDA numbers in the coming years. Bottom line net earnings don't disregard things like taxes, interest paid, or depreciation. Measure if your business is making you money as the owner, and don't simply start focusing on the EBITDA number to run the company. But do keep in mind that if a business loan can help to increase EBITDA numbers before a sale, then it may be a good idea to do so to increase the company valuation.

Of course, being a great CEO is hard work so having to deal with the sale of the business is best left to people who have the knowledge of the process and more importantly the time that it takes to find a buyer, go through the due diligence, and negotiate the best deal. In this instance, much as with my comments about commercial real estate brokers, I caution you to not completely trust a business broker to look out for your interests. Yes, they do get paid a percentage - usually 8-10% - on the sale price of your business, but their desire to have you sell at a higher amount is often overshadowed by their desire to have you sell the business quickly. They are selling multiple companies every month, so their measure of success has more to do with the speed of churn on sales of businesses than getting the best deal for you.

I have been brought in to several companies before a business sale; the largest was for ten figures and the smallest seven figures. In all cases being an independent consultant allowed me to keep any emotions out of the process, while focusing on negotiating the best deal for my client, working with a law firm to draw up sales contracts and related documents, and answer buyer questions without any bias as I had no ownership in the business. In effect I was in a position of being able to help the two parties negotiate with each other, trusting me to bring an unbiased perspective. Ultimately after being paid by the selling client for selling the business, I did work for both the seller and the buyer in the coming months to help the transition go smoothly.

If you can sell your business to your children or other relatives, congratulations! You have saved the cost of a business broker. But you should still plan on spending money for lawyers to draw up a legal contract and for the transition which will ensure that things go as smoothly as possible. Even if you sell to your kids, it is worthwhile to work with a professional to put together the transition plan and be sure that there are no surprises as you wind down your participation in the company.

If you are lucky enough to have the business stay in the family and get a single large payout for it, then you are in the ideal scenario where you can enjoy life and not worry about the business you sold. However most people I have known who have sold their company to their children end up doing a payment plan over time. In effect acting as the bank for their buyer and receiving payments over the course of several years. This may be more stressful than running the business because you are no longer making any strategic decisions in the company, but at the same time, your future payments rely on that business being successful and your relatives being able to afford to pay you on time. Consider what the consequences are if your relatives drive the business into the ground and are unable to pay you. Do you really want to get the assets of your business back at that point?

The bottom line from this chapter is that selling a business is a full-time job. Much as the person who is his own lawyer has a fool for a client, the owner who thinks they can get the most money for their business by selling it without help is guaranteed to be leaving more money on the table than the cost of having someone sell it for them.

II

BOTTOM LINE GROWTH

CONTRACT RENEGOTIATION

IT'S OKAY TO CHANGE YOUR MIND. REALLY.

*W*hen I come in to consult with a business, it is often because the company has been bleeding money in expenses, even if they are good at making sales. One of the first things I look at when I come in is the state of existing business contracts. There are sometimes occasions when a business has poorly executed sales contracts, but that seems to be much less frequent than what I see with expense side contracts.

Whether long-term leases, internet service contracts, outsourced employee contracts or other expense contracts, there is a tendency by most of my clients to just renew the contracts with the terms they were initially drawn up under, without doing a business need review or a competitive bid solicitation for these contracts. Of course, you may have contracts that are favorable to the business, and it is a good idea to keep them at current terms, but quite often what you are getting out of a contractual relationship is not what you expected. In situations like these, it's important not to forget that you can not only ask for better terms during renewal but that you can generally cancel the contract and renegotiate to a better one. In fact, if you want to save money but have no problem with the quality of service, you can often propose a longer-term contract with lower rates or a discount, like several months free.

Another business consultant I know had a project from a client to find unused phone/frame relay/leased lines across 3000 locations. His project cut over $1.3 million in annual telecom spending by negotiating out of contracts which were not being used.

Most contracts will include termination clauses with and without a cause. Termination before end date without cause will generally incur a penalty. Termination with a cause will usually have no penalty but does require the other party be able to fix the issue within some number of days first. Keep in mind though that the legal language in the contract is there in case you go to court to settle a dispute. There is nothing that says that you can not renegotiate a contract midstream without ever going to court. As long as both parties are in agreement, you can make whatever changes you both agree to even if they drastically alter the contract.

So how do I get both parties to agree? Well beyond enforcing a contract, most companies have other priorities like to keep you as a customer or to get positive testimonials from you so they can get more customers. They also often recognize their own problems, and while they prefer that you keep paying the same amount as before these problems became evident, they are generally reasonable in providing discounts or fully renegotiating a contract to remedy the situation.

But what if there are no difficulties and you just don't need the service any longer. Well, in that case, presenting the vendor with good insight as to why you are no longer a good fit will often result in a reduction of terms. Ultimately most companies prefer to change their contract and receive some money from you while providing you fewer services than to spend money on having a wholly canceled contract go to court - with no guarantee of ever being able to enforce it. The buyer always has an advantage in this arena because an unhappy buyer who makes a ruckus on social media is almost always seen as a victim, while the vendor the villain.

While I'm not recommending that you abuse this, it is incredible to see how many of my clients unhappily pay bills for services they do not fully use and yet never consider rene-gotiating. Lastly, keep in mind that there may be deals from other vendors that help you get out of a current contract. I've seen internet providers as well as cell phone companies offer to pay cancellation fees if you move to them and cancel on their competitor. If you have enough lines, they may even provide you free or reduced price equipment which is not offered to the general public. If your COO is too busy to do contract reviews and renegotiations regularly, consider having a consultant come in to help you do this at least once a year.

13

BANKING RELATIONSHIPS

DO WE HAVE A GOOD RELATIONSHIP?

I rarely see a company who has changed banks since it was initially founded. Usually, the founders pick the bank that they already bank at themselves and open up an account for the business. If the company stays small, there is little benefit in looking for other options as the convenience of having a single bank for personal and business is not worth losing. However, not all banks are alike and not all banks are as good this year as the last when it comes to business services. If you have a line of credit with a bank, but you rarely use it, consider: is that because you do not ever need it or because the cost of using it makes it much less useful? Small community banks and credit unions often have very pro-business attitudes. They are proactive in finding SBA programs and ways to help their business customers financially through auxiliary services. So the same banks that are less convenient for personal banking due to limited geography and lack of locations when traveling may be the best banks for your growing business.

Having a business banking relationship with a large bank may not get you much in the way of services even if you do millions in transactions with them. Of course just because a bank is small does not mean it's business friendly either. You will have to do some research or have a consultant do that for you, to see which bank can do more than just hold your money, but also give you a strategic advantage.

I've had several clients who were not even aware of all the banks the company had accounts in because they assumed the CFO was being proactive about managing financial relationships only later to discover that banking decisions were made out of personal convenience and not primarily for the economic benefit of the company.

Keep in mind that banks are probably not the only financial institutions with which you interact. You may be using a third party processing service that specializes in getting you the best rates on credit card transaction processing. Benefits like credit card points provided to the buyer are often recouped by the issuer from additional transaction fees the processor charges you. These processing fees can put a big dent into your bottom line. Good processors will have relationships which will save you money based on the type of business you have and goods sold. They also often have contacts with other service companies which may be useful to you and save you money. Likewise, private lines of credit are often available but not well publicized. Remember, you won't know what relationships could benefit you unless you ask your vendors to make introductions.

While having the best banking relationship will not make or break a company, it is often a neglected aspect which can help bolster the bottom line with reduced fees and provide the most cost-effective loans when cash flow doesn't allow for fast growth.

14

CREDITOR REVIEWS

DO OUR LINES OF CREDIT REALLY MEET OUR NEEDS?

*A*t some point in the growth of a small business, you most likely received a letter from your bank, or maybe a local credit union that offered a $50,000 credit line for your business. That is usually the smallest amount offered. As time went on you probably received progressively larger credit line offers. Using corporate credit cards for travel and other occasional expenses is mostly a matter of convenience and organization. The points don't hurt of course! However, credit lines are meant to be used in much more significant amounts and often business owners don't know when to best utilize them and for what types of expenditures.

As a general rule credit card should be used for expenses which you plan on paying each month fully. Business loans should be used for acquiring long-term assets where the utility of the asset is measured in years. Lines of credit are best utilized for short-term expenses of 60-180 days. An example of proper use of a credit line is to purchase inventory which will be entirely sold within 90-120 days. Inventory should usually not be purchased on a credit card because of their higher interest rates compared to other loans. Non-credit line loans, while providing the best rates, will generally require collateral above and beyond company receivables, so using that to finance inventory is often not practical.

Another good use of a credit line might be to finance equipment that cannot be self-financed out of cash flow but does not require multi-year loans. Having a credit line allows a company to make a discretionary spending decision, but it's essential that the credit line will be used only for expenses that will increase sales or will enable the company to grow within a reasonably short period. Using a credit line for expenditures like marketing or paying employee salaries is usually a reliable indicator of significant financial problems within the company which will only further be compounded by the use of said credit line.

It's important to remember that a credit line is not a lifeline to keep your company afloat when things are going poorly. While it's tempting to do just that, and unfortunately many companies including several past clients have used a credit line as a lifeline, it never ends well. The only sure way of fixing financial problems in business is to be able to reduce expenses while optimizing the efficiency of money spent on generating sales until the sales pick back up. Many companies have gone from multi-million dollar operations to an ungraceful exit by relying too much on credit or loans to sustain them rather than keeping operating costs under control as they grow.

A credit line appropriately used will allow a company to enhance its ability to grow, while a credit line used poorly will add to the instability of a company and may ultimately be responsible for the final nail in the coffin of that company. A strong CFO is vital to ensuring that the temptation to use a credit line is not used for the wrong reasons. A good COO will make sure that activities which incur expenses do not require the company to dip into a credit line unless there is an extremely high likelihood of company growth within a short timeframe as a result of the use of credit.

15

TECHNOLOGY REVIEW

HOW TO DO MORE, FASTER, CHEAPER, AND WITH FEWER PROBLEMS

*T*echnology is a wonderful thing that improves our lives, increases our automation and allows businesses to do more with less. However, it is important to remember that technology cannot solve every problem a company has and quite often business owners want to throw technology at every problem the business encounters. Knowing when to use technology as a solution, when to use people, and how to balance the two optimally is a requirement for a successful CEO, CTO, and COO.

Depending on the size of the business you have, you may be bombarded by technology software and hardware salespeople who will claim to offer products that will do amazing things for your business. Do not become too exuberant about their claims and realize that many tools designed to save time or automate processes will take substantial resources and time to implement. Very often the savings get entirely taken up by the deployment process. I have seen numerous companies struggle with rollout delays as well as products not being

70

able to be implemented due to a lack of understanding of core business processes.

This chapter will be a more extended section because I want to cover a multitude of technology-related services and how you should use them to improve efficiency and profitability.

Let's look at several technologies that are commonly being used successfully to accelerate business.

Cloud-based accounting

In the past accounting systems were generally a decade or more behind all other business software. When Windows 7 came out, people using accounting systems often couldn't upgrade from Windows 98 because the accounting software would break. The user interface of most of the packages both on Mac and Windows was also terribly clumsy. It was as though all the restrictions associated with paper-based journaling were brought into the computer accounting systems, even if there was no good reason for it.

Luckily after 2010, cloud-based accounting systems started popping up which were much more modern. Even Quickbooks had to release their own cloud-based system. Right now there is no reason at all to be stuck on an antiquated accounting system that limits functionality and reporting. All companies, including those making over $100 million annually, are well served to move to cloud-based systems. Finding the right consultant to get you there is the key to a smooth transition. Plan on three months for a small business up to 12 months for a larger company to fully transition.

CLOUD-BASED CRM

Unlike accounting systems, Client Relationship Management (CRM) vendors were early innovators in the cloud revolution, and there were solutions for both larger companies like Salesforce.com and smaller ones like ZenDesk. Even Microsoft has positioned their CRM, Dynamics, as a cloud-based solution, no longer requiring MS Servers to host it.

The critical requirements for a good CRM from an operations perspective are: automation to reduce the need for manual processes by the sales or support departments; and standardization of data, so that every department or employee does not have a unique way of storing client information which makes searching unproductive. A good CRM will force standardization of data while being flexible to fit the business rules. Cloud CRM solutions are no different.

Plan on spending from an additional 50% to 100% the yearly cost of the CRM on a consultant/developer to get the CRM setup correctly for your company. In this instance, the advice is similar to that given by carpenters. Measure twice, cut once. Get everything scoped and architected to fit your business, before starting to build it out.

CLOUD-BASED E-commerce

E-commerce solutions used to involve running specialized software on a locally hosted web server which communicated with the company's credit card processing platform, sometimes via a private leased line connection. This led to all kinds of problems and insecurities. Luckily by the 2010s most of the E-commerce solutions could live in the cloud and securely communicate with processors and banks via the internet. This means that PCI requirements, which are covered in a later chapter, from the company selling the product are decoupled and makes the whole process modular.

Companies like Ultracart, Shopify, and even Amazon offer ways for companies to sell goods and products with full automation and minimal technical knowledge. Some services are so simple that even people without technical skills can set up products for sale. Of course, any complicated sales path or sales of products with custom discounts may still require a consultant to come in and do a one-time setup. In either case, companies can now be online and selling products in days, not weeks or months as was the case previously.

* * *

CLOUD BACKUP and storage

There is not much to say about cloud backup services like Backblaze, Carbonite, or even dropbox.com. All of them give you greater peace of mind by providing incremental backup - sometimes several times per hour - of all your files offsite. This used to be a costly service for companies costing hundreds of thousands of dollars and being used only for the most precious company data. With the fall in prices of both hard disk drives and internet service, the cost of real-time backup to the cloud has dropped to levels where every company and even individual can now afford to have the peace of mind to know their data is safe.

Additionally, services like Dropbox and box.com also allow be used for primary storage and allow multiple computers to sync information, so not only is your data backed up in the cloud but also it is useful for day to day replication of data enabling you to use multiple computers with each having the latest versions of every document auto-matically. When I travel, I know that even if the internet speed is slow, I have a copy of all my files as of the last time the computer connected to the internet. Setting up such a service is so easy now that it does not require an IT person. Although if you want to do a company-wide cloud backup, an IT consultant would be able to help that project complete faster.

I'm a big fan of Dropbox over other similar services because I find that it managed to maintain a minimalist inter-face; it sits in the background and does its job without adding more and more features that most people don't need. The primary role of Dropbox is to synchronize your data across multiple computers, phones, and tablets while also providing a continuous backup of that data to their cloud servers.

You can send any files that you place into your Dropbox to clients, and they will get a link to see a web page with just that file, or if they are also a Dropbox user, they can simply add that folder to their own Dropbox. This is a handy feature because it allows bidirectional document exchange with a client or vendor without clogging up email with multiple versions of Word file, as we used to do in the past.

If you use Box.com or Google One or MS OneDrive, then keep using them. I have all of them as well, but the one I use the most by a long stretch is Dropbox.

FACEBOOK/GOOGLE advertising

While there have always been Advertising Agencies and PR Firms, since the rise of Google ads, Youtube ads, and more recently Facebook ads, there are now specialists who focus on Facebook, Google, or other digital platforms. Companies like Battle Bridge Labs are digital marketing agencies who compliment traditional Ad firms by focusing on bringing the audience from the internet. This involves a specialized skill set which is continually changing and would require a full-time staff to stay on top of the latest changes in digital advertising.

So while anyone can set up a Facebook or Google Ad campaign by merely following the training of companies like Digital Marketer, do keep in mind that your ads are going to be competing with professionally produced marketing campaigns done by agencies who focus on this for a living. The obvious advice here is to outsource digital marketing to a competent digital marketing firm.

Unfortunately, there are many people and small businesses who advertise themselves as digital marketers who are not very good. In fact, they may be very good at doing digital marketing for themselves, but not their clients. Since companies needing help in this area know even less about what to look for, there is often disappointment after a lack of results. The best way to find good assistance in this area is to rely on someone who has used a company and can vouch for their ability to target and convert successfully.

The biggest problem my clients often face is not in finding leads, but rather in controlling costs. If you have the budget for it, you can always get leads, but getting good leads cheaply is the real goal. Finding the right marketing agency to deliver on that will require time and money. So find a good specialist, set up a test budget for them to hone in on the right type of lead, and slowly - yes slowly - increase the ad budget. Never rely on a few examples to determine long-term marketing. Always have a feedback loop that increases the budget as profitability from those leads continues to improve and as importantly decrease your budget if profitability starts to slip. Better to spend a bit more on testing than to lose all your profit on a poor ad buy.

Keep in mind that hiring experts in these areas generally adds some fixed expenses that the business has to cover. Most companies providing these services work on a mix of retainer and commission.

The bottom line is while the technology exists, this is still an area where human knowledge is critical. Paying for expertise will get better results than merely using the technology alone.

CLOUD-BASED email marketing

To support advertising and marketing activities, automated email communication with the client is essential. Throughout the 2000s all but the largest companies generally used their own email server to send out emails to customer lists, but during that time a number of businesses were started which focused on providing commercial email services to other companies. The CAN-SPAM act prompted the shift to outsourcing marketing emails onto specialists. This legislation added many requirements to prevent uncontrolled, unwanted marketing emails from clogging up people's mailboxes. Additionally, large email providers like Google and Yahoo had implemented SPAM filters which often erred on the side of categorizing any commercial email coming in from a non-whitelisted address as SPAM. This meant that many companies who had used their own servers for years to send out marketing to their client lists were now being relegated to SPAM folders for all their email correspondence.

In the past he best way to ensure your email made it to the main inbox was to use a mass commercial email provider company like AWeber, MailChimp, Constant Contact, or companies like Epsilon who service Fortune 500 customers. Today, that is still very much the case. If you plan on using automated email marketing, many companies want your business. Luckily most of them are now also pretty good at importing and exporting list data, so you are not stuck with a particular company if they don't offer the features you need.

Email is still one of the best ways to be engaged with your customers, but keep in mind that people are much better at hitting the unsubscribe button today than they were a decade ago. Keep content relevant, and ask questions with links back to community forums or facebook. This way email will feel less like spam and more like useful communication.

One more recent development that makes marketers lives more difficult is the European GDPR. This European law makes companies responsible for both protecting customer data and for deleting that data if a customer requests it. It potentially adds a layer of complexity to CRM systems that was not needed just a few years ago. This law applies not only to EU companies, but to all companies world wide who have clients who are EU residents.

Cloud-based project management

Project management used to be pretty rare in small companies in the 90s. Back then the Project Management Institute (PMI) was just starting to grow, and the primary tool of PMs was Microsoft Project. While project tools have not evolved as fast as some business tools, they definitely evolved more quickly than accounting tools. Today cloud tools like Mavenlink, Asana, Teamwork.com, or multi-communication tools like Slack all make project management faster and easier. The quality of the tools far outweighs the difficulty in enforcing a culture of project management and accountability at this point. Some tools are better suited to one type of PM methodology than another. For example MS Project is great for Waterfall but not Agile or SCRUM methodologies while tools like Trello are best for Kanban but not for Waterfall. Picking the best tool will depend on which methodology the project manager will use.

Aside from cloud tools, I always recommend that a company send at least one person with project management responsibility to PMI certification classes. While a certification is not required, the ability to understand and communicate standardized project management principles with others is well worth the time and money investment.

* * *

Microsoft Office/Google Docs

Word and Excel used to account for nearly 100% of all business files. But about 15 years ago Google decided to add another option. They created horribly simple word processing and spreadsheet cloud apps. There was no real competition between the Google apps with the market leaders from Microsoft back then. However, as the years passed, Google kept updating and tweaking these apps, eventually even adding a slide presentation cloud app. The ease of use combined with the ability to live edit files so that multiple people can see changes happening in real time is giving the Microsoft products more and more competition. So much so that eventually, Microsoft came out with their own cloud office solution called Office 365. This has a yearly access fee-based solution that provided many of the features of Word and Excel in the cloud. It too was tweaked and expanded unit now there are almost no differences between the cloud version and the native apps on your computer. Apple also put their apps in the cloud calling it iCloud. This never caught on to the extent that Google and Microsoft apps did and most

Apple users I know use either Google or Microsoft cloud solutions.

I still like Google for its much cleaner interface and the fact that it has documents going back a decade for me. Ultimately the question of which to use will be a choice of subscription cost and amount of existing data for most companies. Both are very good, and both can easily exchange files with the other.

BUSINESS INTERNET ACCESS

There has been a lot of consolidation in the Business Internet service provider space. It used to be standard for small businesses to have dozens of options for internet connectivity. Now there are two or three choices, and that is it. AT&T, Comcast, and a couple of other vendors now cover most of the country and thereby limit the choice of vendor. For large companies needing true business-grade connectivity there are many more options as vendors lease lines to each other sometimes creating wild price swings that don't make any sense.

The climate for competition is much worse than it was, luckily prices are still coming down. Or, rather I should say speeds are increasing while prices are holding steady. Where a 10MB connection may have cost $600 a few years ago, now for that price you can get 50 or even 200MB. Since employees expect internet at the office not just for carrying out their work, but for providing connectivity to YouTube, Facebook, and other information centers, it may not feel as though speeds are any faster at the office though!

The bottom line is: negotiate your contract and then re-negotiate it every two years. The odds are that there has been a speed increase or price drop and you will likely be able to get on the new deal, but only if you bother negotiating.

AMAZON CLOUD SERVICES

During the last decade, more and more businesses migrated on Amazon servers. While the servers can do many of the things I've mentioned in this chapter, they can also run the core business intelligence processes and even provide the product your company is selling post sale. Amazon is not the only player in this arena, but they have done a brilliant job of grouping a lot of different cloud-based IT services in a single portal to allow companies to leverage elastic environments that grow and shrink with customer needs in a way that local hardware IT infrastructures could not.

While Amazon services are generally much cheaper than old-style company operated private servers, do keep in mind that Amazon charges for most services by use, rather than a flat fee. This means that the more your clients use a service that you run on Amazon, the higher your monthly bill will be. Ensure that someone is monitoring your costs on at least a monthly basis and that business decisions reflect the ongoing costs. Lastly keep in mind that if your bills from Amazon are in the tens of thousands per month, there is room to negotiate.

For customers at those levels and higher, Amazon will assign a customer rep, and they can evaluate your needs and lower prices, generally in trade for some duration of minimum use contracts. So if you know you will be using the same or more, you could save thousands by working with your Amazon rep. I'm sure other cloud companies are also willing to lower costs for customers doing over $10,000 a month, or maybe even less.

The thing about all cloud services is that you pay a single price for the service. Compare this to the IT of the past where companies had to pay for servers, network gear, electricity, cooling, real estate, carbon offsets for above and labor to keep it running. That doesn't even include the developers that were needed to build applications on top end CRMs. Cloud is simpler, and usually brings a cost reduction.

16

SHIPPING CONTRACT EVALUATION

HOW MUCH TOO MUCH ARE WE PAYING?

*I*f your business sells a shippable product, then you are likely dealing with logistics and associated costs. Shipping solutions from FedEx, UPS, and even USPS are cloud-based and very easy to use in this day. What's important is that all these companies offer volume discounts, but rarely will they offer to reduce your pricing. I recommend having your COO and not a shipping manager negotiate shipping rates and try to do that on a yearly basis as your volume of shipped goods grows.

There are also other shipping options available to volume shippers, like DHL, which are not available to small volume needs so consulting with someone who is knowledgeable in that space is going to allow you to be sure that cost of shipping is as little as possible. If you are not yet large enough to get discounts through existing volume, you should look for a shipping aggregator or a logistics company like FedEx GENCO or ShipWire. These types of companies, called Third Party Logistics (3PL), can become an outsourced fractional warehouse so that you do not have to lease your facility. They can provide outsourced warehouse staff. They can also negotiate better shipping rates using their volume discounts.

If you ship internationally, Customs Brokers can help with the import or export process and provide Customs management to ensure a smoother and cheaper transfer through the customs office. With no prior experience, the process can become expensive because the right forms were not filed. Finally having expertise in different types of insurance depending on the risk factors associated with different countries.

The bottom line is that you can probably hire a third party logistics company and pay for all their services entirely out of the money saved on shipping and warehousing, assuming you are doing over $3 million per year in sales.

17

REDUCTION OF LEGAL FEES

AGAIN, HOW MUCH TOO MUCH ARE WE PAYING?

*E*veryone knows lawyers are expensive. However, when you need a lawyer, you feel more confident in using one that is expensive because the more expensive a lawyer, the better the lawyer. At least that's how many people's thinking goes.

In my experience, there are good expensive lawyers, but also good budget lawyers, as well as expensive bad lawyers. If the hourly rate is not a guarantee of quality, then is there a reason to use an expensive, prestigious law firm? Yes and no! Rather than basing the selection of a firm on their rate, I find it's more important to evaluate the attorney who will handle your corporate needs individually and be sure that their values reflect yours. For example, there is no need to add more stress to your life by having an attorney who is more aggressive and litigious than the business owner. However, equally, a CEO who is happy to use legal means to ensure the company rights are enforced should not have to continually be convincing his attorney to press harder, file sooner, and pursue all available legal action. The temperament of the lawyer handling the company business should be congruent with that of the owner or CEO. Their job should be to remove issues off the corporate leadership plate, not to pile more on.

So if you found a lawyer you are comfortable with, how do you save money then? Well, their rate is their rate, and I would not try to negotiate that. However, there are a couple of things a business can do to reduce overall legal costs - depending on the size of the business. In larger companies, it may actually prove to be more cost effective to hire corporate counsel in a salaried position. In this case, you would like still spend $200,000-500,000 per year on that role, but unless there are significant lawsuits, external legal fees should be vastly reduced unless you go to trial. For smaller companies, this is overkill and not a good option.

The advice I am about to give you is not legal advice, and it likely would be argued against by lawyers, including my friends, but having been the point of contact for working with law firms on behalf of many companies over the last 20 years, it is what I've found works best to reduce fees. Here is the advice - for non-litigious matters such as contracts, it is much, much cheaper to use people who do not have an ESQ behind their name, but who routinely work to draft and update legal documents. Hiring a part-time or even full-time person with ten years of paralegal experience is much cheaper and will get you 90% of the way in most business legal issues which do not involve lawsuits.

Most businesses who have a law firm on retainer will rely on the firm to create contracts for various business arrangements. What the company does not realize is that in the law firm a paralegal will copy and past the majority of the contract from past similar agreements, or simply use a template that the firm has for similar contracts. They will then customize the contract based on your requirements, and send it to a lawyer in the firm for final proof. The amount of time spent by someone without a law degree on your work will be 90% or more, with 10% or less involving someone who passed the state bar exam. So rather than paying $300/hr for that 90%, it is much easier for that portion to be done in-house by someone competent in the law, but not certified in it. The remaining 10% or less will still be done by your law firm.

From my experience with multiple clients, a Non-Disclosure and Indemnification agreement has cost $2800-$4500 directly from a law firm. The same type of document created in-house using templates and then edited by someone familiar with legal language will take 2-3 hours with a likely cost of $300 or less. A law firm will still do the final inspection and tweaks, but just an hour or two of actual lawyer time at the cost of $300-$600. So $2,800-$4,500 vs. $600-$900 is a difference that is hard to ignore. Other contracts, business agreements, or employee termination notices result in similar percentage savings.

There are some caveats of course. The person doing the editing of the documents should have both a good understanding of the business needs and of state and federal laws relating to this kind of document. I would absolutely not advise a business owner merely to find templates using google and change the company name. If used without a legal review, there will likely be items missing or clauses that are not applicable to the company. Moreover, if sent to the law firm, you will probably not get much of savings as they will effectively need to re-write the document. This savings only works if you have access to a resource who is knowledgeable about the law, but is cheaper because they did not have to pass the bar. The other caveat is for any matters involving litigation, where a state bar registered attorney will be required. Although in this case, it is good to have someone familiar with legal requirements and ramifications be assigned to work with the law firm to ensure the priorities of the business represented best by the law firm.

Since this chapter is all about saving money on legal expenses, it would not be complete without covering the topic of insurance as well. There are many insurance options that businesses can buy. A very common choice is Errors and Omissions insurance. The intent of this coverage is to protect the business against lawsuit expenses in case of customer lawsuits. Quite often the first action your company lawyer will take in instances where you are notified of an intent of a lawsuit is to contact your insurance company and open up a case. The insurance company will have a lawyer work on their behalf to either settle with the disgruntled party and payout or to fight and take the case to court. Of course, there are many more intricacies there, but having insurance that covers certain kinds of actions will minimize the company's exposure to lawsuits.

Additionally, there other legal insurances available which do not cover the cost of settling or losing the case but do include the legal fees of certain types of incidents so that these legal costs do not all show up unexpectedly in one month. For example, I have seen insurance that covers legal fees, usually up to a certain limit, of HR-related cases which require legal engagement. A variant of this is legal insurance for your employees which does not directly save the company money, but does provide a benefit for your employees and reduces the stress level for them in case of legal issues.

I will give you a personal example of this type of insurance. I had been working for a huge multinational, and they had what I later termed Divorce Insurance - which covered legal fees associated with getting divorced. Divorce is a massive drain on both parties and very often reduces savings to nothing. Having your employees not have to deal with the added stress of paying tens of thousands in legal fees on top of the stress of going through a divorce means the company has a less distressed employee who is still able to concentrate on their job during divorce. When I first found out about this benefit upon starting the job, I thought it was ridiculously funny and a statement about the divorce rate in the US. Several years later when I was going through my own divorce, I thought it was a godsend. Having my legal fees covered by this company covered insurance during the divorce also helped the divorce settlement be equitable because my ex-wife knew that the longer the divorce stretched, the more expensive it would be for her, but not for me. In the end, my legal bills were lower, and I believe the divorce concluded quicker than it would have otherwise. This, of course, had the desired result for the employer as my focus was on work matters with minimal interruption for the divorce and no stress from legal bills.

To summarize my advice, I suggest you find a law firm that reflects your level of legal demeanor, whether aggressive or conservative, utilize cheaper resources where it does not compromise quality, and look at legal insurance options to reduce future unplanned costs.

18

STAFF REDUCTION

THE RIGHT TEAM FOR TODAY MIGHT NOT BE YESTERDAY'S TEAM

*I*f you've worked in a traditional corporate ladder-climbing environment, you already know that some employees seem to get fast-tracked and others stagnate in their roles and may even get ushered out. In case you need more details, I cover the "Up or Out" strategy in depth in Business Growth Roadblocks, my previous book. If you are not familiar with that, I suggest you go to Amazon right now and get a copy! (I'll wait right here) In a nutshell, your employees should grow, change, and mature with the company to fill higher roles, or they should leave. Howard H. Stevenson from Harvard Business School said it well.

> "There's a difference between 20 years of experience, and one year of experience 20 times."

All too often management at every level including CEOs

think that the longer an employee is with the company, the more that speaks to how well the company is managed. The reality is entirely different. It can actually demonstrate poor staff development, because too low a turnover can often be an even bigger problem. The quote above speaks to that issue. Having employees with a year's worth of experience repeated over and over is not only a detriment to personal development, but also hinders business growth.

But in this chapter let's assume you understand the need for pruning your company tree and look at the best way to do that. The first step that I go through when looking for opportunities to reduce HR costs, aka laying off staff, is to look at the extended salary costs. It may surprise some readers, but I don't merely look at the performance of staff divided by costs. I also look at the impact that an immediate layoff will make on the bottom line and divide that by the effect on the company. So I'm not only looking at reducing costs based on removing the least producing staff, but also on the greatest impact to the bottom line costs. This means that I often cut a single highly paid person ahead of a couple of lower-priced employees. Everything else being equal, firing someone working in a lower paying job will have a much smaller impact on cost savings - so this is often not the best place to start looking for cuts.

With one recent client, I had a situation where the company had too low a revenue to support the staff they had. After interviewing everyone, I knew we would need to lay off some employees, so I had put together my list. It was comprised of employees and contractors who were either duplicating roles or who at this point in the company were overqualified (and overpaid) for the company needs. Unfortunately, this included people who were hired for the needs of a future growing company and were very underutilized as the company had shrunk. Among this group was an HR director who I was very impressed with during my interview with her. She was very helpful to my researching the company during the project, and it was a sad irony that someone I considered one of the most talented people in the company would have to be on my list of cuts. But as I often remind myself, I work for the client to help ensure the success of the business as my primary goal.

As the timeline for cuts was getting closer, I had to work with her as the HR director to walk her through the other people who would be let go. She not only understood my rationale for the cuts but also understood the methods because she had read my last book. A day after our conversation, she came to my office and asked if she was on the list to be cut as well. I had to admire her perception and confirmed that she was. She then asked if she could work through the last day. I had told her I planned on allowing people not show up for the last week after letting them know they were being laid off. She wanted to finish out her job through the last day and help with the transition of all those folks. Once again my level of respect for her increased, but that did not change that the best thing for the company was to let an overqualified person go. True to her professionalism, none of the other employees suspected that she was also leaving as she was walking the other layoffs through HR forms and making sure the transition of their jobs was seamless for the company.

You may be wondering if I ended up letting her go in the

end. I did indeed. But, I found her a job at another company where her talents could be better utilized, and she would have a higher role. She interviewed at that job two days after her last day of work, and before the week was out, she already had an offer for a new and better job. Total time unemployed was less than five days. So, when people ask me if I feel bad about laying off people at every client I work with, I say I actually feel good about helping people transition to better fitting jobs, even if sometimes they don't immediately see it that way.

While letting people go is not fun and is often avoided, it should not be the last ditch effort to save a business or improve profitability. As I mentioned in chapter five above, routinely reviewing the performance of your employees when things are going well will help ensure that the company is always getting the most benefit from employees and contractors. This, in turn, should help keep the company profitable and not force it to have to cut payroll under duress.

If you look at successful modern companies, like GE, Amazon or Tesla you can see that they both cut non-performing employees and aggressively fill needed roles. As I write this book, Tesla just laid off 400 people after finishing internal performance reviews. Many of those laid off were management including senior positions. At the same time, Tesla still has over 2000 open job listings waiting to be filled due to its growth. In being proactive about performance reviews and not being afraid to lay off underperforming staff, Tesla ensures that the company as a whole stays healthy and focuses on profit and innovation.

19

CONTRACTOR REVIEW

HOW MANY NON-EMPLOYEES ARE YOU PAYING? AND WHY?

"You've got to know when to hold 'em

Know when to fold 'em

Know when to walk away

And know when to run"

— THE GAMBLER BY KENNY ROGERS

---

*E*very business can benefit from using contractors - instead of, and sometimes in addition to, full-time employees. In my experience, few business leaders understand in which cases you should use contractors and when you should hire employees. Maybe because that topic is not taught as much as it should be, in most companies I've worked with the division of roles between employees and contractors is often determined merely by the availability of staff at some point in time. I've seen companies who couldn't afford a full-time developer maintain contract developers who were being paid more than equivalent full-time staff for multiple years. I've also seen the opposite situation when there were full-time staff in roles the company once needed to be full time, but only needs past time now. Like with many topics in this book, the lesson is to be proactive rather than reactive.

The main reason for hiring someone as a non-employee or a contractor is because it enables you to get a level of talent or specialization for the company on a less than full-time or short-term basis which you otherwise could not afford or do not require long term. There are both Federal and State definitions of what legally distinguishes a contractor from an employee. In general, if they are doing specialized work, are in charge of their own time, working for a short duration, and are not directly supervised, then you should use a contractor. If, on the other hand, you find that you are using a contractor full-time and do not expect to end their role any time soon then it likely will make more financial sense to find an employee to fill that role. In fact, using a contractor while searching for an employee is an excellent use of contractors.

Within the term contractor, there are several possible definitions. The simplest is what is generally known as staff augmentation. In that scenario, a business needs additional short-term staff, and a contractual relationship with a staffing company can provide that staff. The second definition of a contractor is when a company needs a specialized service that it does not have the in-house capabilities of doing. For example, many companies contract out the installation and configuration of their computer networks or specialized machinery. A specialist will come in and provide the services to do the installation and train your regular staff. At that point, the day to day maintenance may be provided by an in-house department, or it may be a full-service contract where the contracted company not only installs the equipment but also maintains it for some duration of time. Another example of contractors may be legal, financial, or, like myself, operations consultants. Many times a consultant will be provided by consulting firms under a contract. Consultants may be employees of the consulting firm, or in turn contractors to the consulting firm. Or they may be independent contractors who are providing consulting services under their own name. This category may also include graphic designers, sales consultants, marketing consultants, or similar services.

Consultants are contractors, but not all contractors are consultants. Generally, the thing that separates consultants, from the broader term contractor, is their specific subject matter expertise within a category which the business wants to utilize for a particular end result. Consultants help a company do something it does not have the strategic knowledge and resources to do alone - they don't have the ability to set the example for the way the business should do this function for the future. Non-consultant contractors are usually not focused on setting strategy or knowledge transfer into the business, but instead, they are focused on executing some specific tactical task or project with the skills the company lacks.

For contractors, this is sort of like the Gambler by Kenny Rogers. So with all those definitions and overlapping terms when should a business use contractors let's follow the song lyrics.

KNOW WHEN TO HOLD 'EM:

You should hold the contractors when there is no immediate transition plan for the business to move to have employees executing the function of the contractor. This can be planned, as in the case of a one-time accounting system installation. Or it may be unplanned when a contract software developer is working on a time-sensitive piece of code, and you have not been able to find a full-time employee developer to fill that role.

> *Caution: Don't just hold 'em because of indecisiveness or inertia - make sure you're actively managing these resources and continue to get good value from the investment. Precisely because of their skill level and reduced direct supervision, it's easy for contractors to get complacent and simply milk the customer as long as possible.*

KNOW WHEN TO FOLD 'EM:

Folding contractors is where most management trips up in my experience. Much as owners and managers tend to hold on to employees too long to avoid having to go through the pain of retraining, so do they tend to hold on to contractors too long to avoid having to make any changes. The problem with contractors, of course, is that you are always paying a premium for the same level of skills in a contractor as you would for an employee. The reason for this is simple, either you are paying that premium for the more uncertain work future for the contractor or you are paying for a more significant set of skills. In either case, if the need you have is a long-term need, having that need filled by a contractor is always a more expensive prospect. Because your goal as a business executive is to maximize profit and increase optimization of the business, you should always have an end date in mind for every contractor working for the company. Some will have the end date spelled out in a contract while others will need to have their contracts terminated once an employee who can take over is found, or if the need goes away. It is management's responsibility, as much as employee reviews, to ensure that contractors get wrapped up as soon as it is feasible for the company.

Caution: Make sure your staff are ready to pick up where the contractor leaves off. You might want to terminate the contractor to reduce cost, but your employees might be left holding the bag for a project they're not prepared or qualified to complete. Moving the contractor to a limited duration part-time engagement to ease the transition is much better for employee morale than having to bring the contractor back in after a failed transition.

* * *

KNOW WHEN TO WALK AWAY:

I've come into many companies where contractor relationships were so one-sided that it was vital to wean the company off that contractor as soon as possible. Generally, this happens when a contractor relationship was established with a variable compensation amount rather than a fixed one. For example, a company needs to have a sales channel managed but lacks skill in managing that channel internally. They find a contractor that has experience to manage it. Since there will be relatively low volume of sales anticipated for the first few months of the relationship, a rate significantly high enough to get someone interested is offered. However as the channel matures and sales keep increasing, this contractual relationship becomes a problem. I've seen contractors that do not have even close to full-time work, yet bill 3X the cost of a full-time, qualified person, doing the same work simply because the person who negotiated the deal didn't have the business knowledge to write a contract with limiting clauses that would allow the company to reduce the percentages paid as volume increased.

KNOW WHEN TO RUN:

Another real-life example for me was a company that employed developers offshore, who had intimate knowledge of the product and demanded more and more money every year. Sad to say, the result of this was the company ended up paying each contractor, what turned out to be, over 20X the average salary for their country. Yes, you read that correctly,

20X of the average wage in the country. In fact, these guys were making so much money they lived in lavish houses, played polo and vacationed for months while having their low wage employees do the work they were hired to do. Since they were offshore in a rather low wage country, the company did not enjoy any cost savings by using offshore labor, but was still able to pay them because they charged about what a US-based contractor would charge. This situation got to where it was because there was no focus in the early stages to find employee replacements for the contractors. Unfortunately these situations all end the same way. Ending the relationship with the vendor is unavoidable in my experience.

In my experience of outsourcing over the last 20 years, the return on foreign labor at this time is never close to the return on domestic labor. Time lost in communication, dealing with different customs and misunderstandings, not to mention the plethora of holidays that most countries outside the US have, make offshore much less attractive than proponents would like to have you believe.

ELIMINATION OF OBSOLETE FEES AND SUBSCRIPTIONS

DO YOU CHECK RECURRING BILLS MONTHLY?

*B*usinesses are not that different from individuals in this regard. People often don't notice and as a result, don't cancel subscriptions or auto-renewing fees for services they no longer use. Some companies build their entire business models on the assumptions that their customers will likely forget to cancel for a few months resulting in more income for the company. While I'm not here to judge the merits of that practice, I do want to be sure that my clients don't suffer from these practices against them. To that end, one of the things I do about midway through a consulting engagement is to review all existing contracts and then analyze all incoming invoices for the last few months. During that process, I almost always discover unused services that the company has been paying for but no longer uses. In fact, sometimes it never used those services.

Remember, the primary job of the accounting department is to receive all the money for the products and services that the company provides and pay all the bills the company incurs as part of its operation. Part of the job of the CFO is to verify that purchases the company makes are legitimate and needed for the operation of the business. But the CFO is not an expert in every other department, so the legitimacy check should be asking the department manager for whom this product or service is to be provided if this is something they approve. I will say from experience that every unused service and product I found was definitely approved at the time of original purchase because assumptions were being made on the future use of it.

So I've absolved the blame from the CFO, but not all intentions are fulfilled according to plan so expenses which were once justified and approved should not be cut. Unfortunately most companies do not have any plan to review existing monthly spending.

My job as an operational efficiency consultant is to look at all those costs and not only check if management approve this, but also push back and ask if the needs can be met some other way. Generally, they can be through some other means. Of course, while I'm working with a client, I also do this for new spending requests as well. Having the benefit of 20 years of hindsight, I can often identify poor spending and stop it in its tracks long before thousands of dollars are wasted.

My experience definitely helps me do this, but even without the experience, requiring a cost-benefit analysis as part of any new spending will go a long way in preventing frivolous spending. Going through the costs and potential benefit that the expenditure will provide before spending any money will help to find projects that seem overly expensive. It will also establish a baseline against which that project costs, can be measured.

Measuring business performance is the first step in making any positive change in the business. Measuring business performance continuously and making small improvements, the way W. Edward Deming taught and which is the basis of Kaizen, is the next step to having a truly successful company.

21

BUDGET INVESTIGATION BY DEPARTMENT

RIGHT-SIZING DOESN'T ALWAYS MEAN SMALLER

*H*aving spent much of the book so far on reducing costs, I want to be very clear that sometimes the most effective course of action is to increase cost - if a commensurate benefit can be gained with acceptable risk. Before I can help a company review individual department budgets, I first have to work with a company that actually does departmental budgeting. It is still sometimes surprising how large a business can become without following sound business practices like having annual or quarterly budgets for departments. It may be common, but please do not translate that into any encouragement to skip the budgeting process. The only thing not having departmental budgets demonstrates is a CEO who does not empower his management. Of course, it also means that a given manager is no longer accountable for their department's success.

Departmental budgets allow the business to measure income and expenses on a per department level and provide the ability to project business performance to match financial goals. Seeing how a company is doing financially gives you a snapshot into the overall performance of the business. But that image may be hiding a great success within one department which is overshadowed by a substantial failure in another department. Yes, it is essential to know the big picture view of a company, but it is no less important to look at the departmental view of the business to see where money is coming in and where it is being spent. If one department is deemed a cost center, then having a complete budget helps determine budgets for revenue generating departments. If a department is supposed to be revenue neutral, measuring actual performance against a budget will raise a flag quickly if costs start to blow past income. As I said in a previous chapter, measuring business performance is the first step in making any positive change in the business.

If your company is under $5 million per year in sales and already budgeting then congratulations, you are in a small group of companies poised on success! But as the chapter title suggests, budgeting is about right-sizing the budget to maximize business performance. It is not about cutting everything to the bone, nor about outlandish spending on items that will have little or no positive impact on the bottom line. Budgeting is an exercise in careful consideration and prioritization of expenses that will have the most likely positive outcome for the company. Every company will have some similarities within budgets for the same departments, but what separates one company from the next is their unique sales proposition. Whether service or product, every company strives to show how they are different and what unique benefit that difference provides to their customers. Likewise, every company should have differences in its budget priorities.

You can find sample departmental budgets online. If you are not budgeting at all, or if you are simply leaving it up to the CFO to fill in projected budget numbers without the full involvement of the department head, then it is an excellent first step to review examples. If you are further along in budgeting, you will always benefit from a budget review performed by a business consultant to compare your department budgets to other companies in similar industries.

22

THE UPS AND DOWNS OF INTERNS

SHOULD WE BE USING THEM?

*I*nternship programs can date their history to apprenticeships, which have been around for over 2000 years. In many jobs, an apprenticeship was the only way to learn the skills necessary get into a trade. Unlike apprenticeships, internships are exclusively for white collar jobs. It is not so much about learning a trade as it is about learning about the way companies operate. An internship can certainly be with one department or even one person in a company, but practically speaking it's about learning how to do that person's job by helping that person with some light tasks and in the process getting a feel for what it might be like to eventually do their job.

I'm a big fan of using interns to augment staff needs and possibly find future full-time employees in the process. I've hired interns for most of the companies I have consulted for in the last decade. In fact, in my previous book, I refer to interns as the secret weapon. Although interns usually come to a company with minimal applicable experience, they have several characteristics which make them very desirable. By the way, when I say, interns, I'm generally talking about 18-23-year-olds either in college or recently graduated. To be sure there can be older interns, but my experience has been with this demographic.

Unlike a summer job at the mall, an internship candidate will be applying for an internship at a company in an industry they have an interest in or are wanting to get into. So right from the point of applying they are more interested in this internship job than other jobs they could get. They have probably recently taken classes related to the industry and learned skills they can apply during the internship. Their knowledge is not in-depth, but it is also less spread out. Meaning if they are a graphic design major, they have taken classes in the Adobe products but probably didn't learn traditional pre-computer design methods, other than perhaps in a historical context. So quite often I found that interns' technical skills were quite good but, as expected, lacking experience. Having grown up with computers and cell phones, they are very familiar with using cloud-based tools and often see faster ways of doing tasks using those tools than older employees. Interns also are very receptive to being trained on new methods of doing things. They have been in schools for over 15 years and are very used to people older than themselves teaching them how to do things. Teaching company methodologies to an intern is generally a much faster process with less resistance than an employee who has more experience and has to be convinced that the company way is a better way to do things. Lastly, interns are just beginning their professional careers. They have no baggage associated with their jobs, no resentments from being passed up for promotions, no broken dreams of success, no political interoffice games. Interns are as close to a blank canvas as you can get in an employee.

Of course, there are some negatives about interns as well. Reliability is probably at the top of my list. Based on the last decade of hiring nearly 75 interns, I would say that over half of them have been MIA for at least one day of work, only to return later as though nothing was wrong. And a good 25% have disappeared from their jobs, never to return again. I think this is related to a lack of social maturity and is precisely how they act with friends as well, not just work. It may also be different in other countries where social maturity occurs much earlier than in the US. Aside from leaving jobs, interns are often prone to show adverse reactions with rising levels of stress than other workers and may also be too timid to bring up problems when they arise. These negatives can be mitigated, and I believe the positives outweigh the negatives overall. The ability of the interns to do good quality work, willingness to go above and beyond, and desire to learn, combined with a very low cost, makes them a great addition to businesses of any size.

During the last decade, I have usually paid interns $10/hr. I based this number on wanting to be slightly above what they could earn in service jobs at the mall so adjust that number for your local rates. Unpaid internships exist, but I've never felt that a company can get the same level of interest and commitment if an intern doesn't see a financial reward tied to their work. Also, free internships usually require the company to do a plethora of paperwork so the intern can get credit at their school. I would rather get them used to earning money for their work. At this point, minimum wage in some states has risen over $10/hr, so where necessary, I would simply bump the intern pay rate to $15/hr. This rate will be higher than my first full-time job pay after college - good old inflation! I've also had a self-imposed rule that interns who are in college can not work more than 20 hours per week on the internship. I don't want to be responsible for bad grades due to lack of sleep!

In my experience about 1 out of 10 interns brought on ends up being such a good performer that they are worth hiring full-time as soon as they graduate. These interns work harder, are more flexible and are quick studies - enabling them to pick up work from existing employees and often execute it at much faster speed, although generally with a few more mistakes. My standard offer to an intern for a permanent position is about 4X of their intern paycheck, depending on prevailing starting wages. What I mean is that if they worked 20 hours at $10 per hour I would hire them at $20 per hour for 40 hours per week, resulting in a 4X of their previous monthly paycheck. Basically, I try to leave room for fast pay increases as long as they keep performing at a high level. Bringing a 22-year-old at the same pay as someone with a decade of experience, even if they can do the work in the same time, is problematic because young employees expect more frequent pay increases. Bringing them in at the top end of the scale will end up frustrating them when they don't get a raise every six months as their friends do. Even if they are very good at the job they now learned to do, they will almost always need more guidance because any deviation from the norm is brand new to them. So reward fresh, enthusiastic employees and motivate them to get better with frequent small bumps in pay, but don't forget the value of seasoned employees who have learned hard lessons in their years of experience - which the youngsters don't yet know.

I can remember two interns over the last decade who were head and shoulders above their peers in showing dedication, willingness to learn and professionalism. Both of them were offered permanent positions, and both of them came aboard as employees. In one case, the company got about 2.5 years out of the former intern before she was let go when her quality of work started to suffer. To the best of my recollection, she had been an excellent employee for about a year and then started spending more time with a couple of employees who were bitter and resentful about their lack of advancement within the company. That negative attitude is a poison pill for the whole office, including interns. I advise letting disgruntled employees go as soon as possible before otherwise good employees start getting corrupted. That is what happened in this case, as she started taking longer smoking breaks, being late to work, ignoring customers and exhibiting other indications of poor performance.

The other intern who was hired was a workaholic videographer. She was great in every regard until she started dating the senior video editor that worked for the company. We initially thought she would replace him and we would hire another intern to train with her. Once she started dating him, her work hours became strictly 9-5, and the speed of work slowed down. The company could not fire him and promote her because she would quit if we fired him, so the company had to live with a diminished quality and speed of work for about a year at which point both of them gave notice at the same time and quit. The lesson learned here may be to have an HR policy about dating who you report to, but ultimately the lesson is to nip problems in the bud by replacing employees who show a decline in performance within 90 days. Although accused of being cutthroat,Amazon has demonstrated this type of policy and uses it very successfully to grow and has become the dominant retail company in the US.

It may sound harsh, but as I've said here and in my last book, I've never met anyone who I fired who wasn't eventually happier and a better worker at a different company. Employees that are performing poorly for the company, are also probably not getting what they need from the company. Giving them the freedom to move on and find a position that will provide them with more of what they need is a positive thing for both the employee and the company.

III

LEGAL AND COMPLIANCE

23

HOW TO USE CONTRACTS TO DEFINE REQUIREMENTS

HOW TO AVOID HARD FEELINGS

*A*s we get into the section dealing with Contracts and Legal topics, let me once again repeat that nothing in this book is offered as *legal advice* and should not be construed as such. What I'm providing is business advice. Always consult your attorney for legal advice.

I think this is a chapter your lawyer will agree with. I want to encourage you to use more contracts in the course of your business. You may already be using contracts for vendors, for non-disclosure agreements, even for non-compete agreements, but having worked with a multitude of companies either threatened with legal action or in the middle of lawsuits, I recommend using contracts far more than most companies use them.

A contract is merely a voluntary arrangement that is documented and is enforceable by law as a binding legal agreement. While there may be verbal contracts, they are usually worth less than the paper they are printed on. For this chapter when I refer to contracts, I'm referring to written contracts, preferably reviewed by lawyers. I have worked in contract dispute resolution cases with clients, and in most instances, the vagueness of language within the contract was the cause of the dispute. One party though it meant one thing, the other party though it meant something else. Each thought their perspective was the one the contract represented. Vague contracts are almost worse than no contracts because they bolster a sense of conviction for both parties who can not understand why the other side sees things so incorrectly.

It is easy to determine what types of arrangements and relationships should be contractually defined because disputes rarely arise if there is no financial remedy. So let's start with the most common contracts, those defining sales and purchasing arrangements. Whether you sell products or services, you can remove any ambiguity from your sales by use of a sales contract. If you sell products through a reseller such as Amazon, they already have a contract that you need to agree with and sign which spells out each of your responsibilities and obligations as well as theirs. With a company as large as Amazon, your products would need to represent a pretty large volume of sales for them to agree to modify their contract with you. But I'm sure there are a few companies who have unique contracts with Amazon, not available to most vendors.

However, if you are selling the same items through a smaller reseller such as Touch of Modern, then you are much more likely to negotiate a change in the contract successfully. If you are selling products directly to a consumer, you should have terms of purchase or terms of service which spell out your rights and obligations as well as the consumers. Keep in mind that consumers have legal protection against specific practices as defined by both federal and state or even city level. Any contractual agreements will have lower precedence than regulatory controls and case law if the dispute goes to court. For this reason, you may have noticed more companies including private binding arbitration clauses in their contracts. By doing this it is essentially keeping disputes out of government courts and using arbitration to resolve them faster. This also allows the entire proceeding to be kept out of the public arena. To boil it down, when you sell something, it is wise to enumerate your rights and obligations, and get agreement from the buying party before the transaction is completed.

Now the flip side of this is when you are the buyer. Whether you are buying raw materials for your products, buying internet access for the office, or buying a service your company will use, it is important to have contracts that define the expectations of each party, reserve your rights and spell out the obligations. If you are dealing with AT&T for your internet services, you will likely have no opportunity to modify a contact. Your negotiations will have to be based on the cost of service while selecting the minimum requirements you are willing to live with. But in executing a contract for the same type of service from a small local ISP, you have much more flexibility in actually modifying the contract and getting favorable terms. Even if the main contract is not open for modification, remember that you can request some specific requirements be spelled out in a schedule or an addendum attached to the contract. It never hurts to see if you can customize the terms.

When it comes to getting services or goods from smaller companies, or any companies where your purchase will be considered a significant sale for them, your ability to create or modify a contract is wide open. I've completely renegotiated and written new agreements for companies when I realized that they represent a substantial buyer to the vendor. Getting more favorable terms, lowering cost, or restructuring the entire deal can be done when you represent a significant volume of sales to the vendor. For this reason, before the company signs any contracts with non-Fortune 500 vendors, it's beneficial to learn enough about the vendor to determine how valuable your contract will be to them. Looking at a list of existing clients is often sufficient to establish that.

For contracts with individuals, the company will most likely need to provide them with a contract, even if the services they are delivering are very valuable to the company. This is not about bullying the vendor to get what you want, but rather that an individual does not need to consult anyone to make unique contractual arrangements, so there is always more flexibility. Negotiating with a company generally involves more people at multiple levels than negotiating with the individual that will be doing the work. The danger, in this case, is that an individual may rely on emotion more when negotiating a contract. The bottom line is when negotiating with a very small company or an individual, you can structure a contract in a way which is generally harder and takes longer for larger companies. Take advantage of this benefit when dealing with small companies.

Now let's look at areas where contracts are less common but which may still be beneficial. When I am hiring a new employee for a company I like to provide a buffer for the company to be able to determine their competence by having them be a temporary employee, or even an independent contractor as long as it does not break employment laws, for an initial period. So even if you do not have employment contracts, having a contract with new hires for an initial period is wise. As a general rule of thumb, I find 60 days is sufficient time to determine if an employee will live up to the way they presented themselves during the interview. Some companies do 90 days, but I've never needed more than 60 to see if someone is a good fit, competent worker, and interacts positively with existing employees. During this trial period, all expectations and requirements can be spelled out with minimal ambiguity. Knowing that they are on track will make the new employee more confident and as a result a more effective employee. This type of Contract to Hire arrangement is more common in technology positions than other positions, because in that role, it's often impossible to fully evaluate a prospect's capabilities without having them actually demonstrate real-world skills while on the job for a while.

Companies will have areas of the business where they are less likely to have contracts in place. For some companies, providing services to sister companies may be an exception to having contracts. For other companies, it may be that the CEO likes to have handshake deals with business partners and doesn't like the idea of contracts. But for almost all companies I've worked with, contracts were not utilized to the full benefit of the company. If it's worth working with another company, it is worth having a well-defined contract describing that relationship.

24

ASSESSING RISK

IS THE POTENTIAL RETURN WORTH THE RISK?

I started my business career in IT while I was in college and from that moved on to Security, then to Regulatory Compliance Auditing, and finally business process improvement. During the mid part of my career, I spent a lot of time analyzing and reducing risk. Whether compliance requirements were based on government regulations or contractual agreements, the quantification of risk was an integral part of the audit process. Even now I bring the concept of acceptable risk to every project for new clients.

Risk Value for our purposes can be defined as the probability that an outcome will be an undesired one multiplied by the negative consequences of that outcome. So you may have an unlikely risk, but with a high price tag, or a more likely risk with a lower price. The net result from these may be the same over time.

Reward Value is the opposite. It is the probability of the desired outcome multiplied by the positive consequences of that outcome. Obviously, the goal of most decisions should be to reduce risk, while increasing the reward. However, although there are many ways to control and reduce risk, there may be risks which are hard to identify without in-depth analysis. For this reason, a culture within the company which incorporates risk analysis into overall operations allows the CEO to make the most informed decisions about the path the company will take.

Some of my clients are much more risk-averse than others, and so my recommendations and the way I restructure the company have to be based on their acceptance of risks. Whether the risks are financial, legal, or competitive, almost every decision made in business carries some risk with it. Learning how to identify, analyze, and manage risk are unfortunately not skills most business owners have spent much time developing. However, these skills, if learned by CEOs create a massive advantage in guiding the business through a competitive landscape. I'm not saying that the CEO is the person to actually do all the risk analysis, but rather setting the expectation that risk analysis will be an integral part of operations while the CEO should communicate to management what acceptable risk tolerance should be at this point in the business.. Any new service or project proposal should include a cost-benefit analysis as well as a risk assessment. This should be the case on a high level for transformative projects for the company as well as on a finer scale for departmental projects. When a risk value is assigned to every project, the executive team can set priorities and create a plan for the company with acceptable risk.

How difficult is it to integrate routine risk assessment into a company? Luckily, assessing risk is not that hard and once employees are exposed to examples of evaluating risk on projects in their departments, they will likely pick up the process fairly quickly. The real key is to maintain this practice at all levels in the organization. Keep in mind that most employees will quickly stop doing work they do not see management utilizing. As long as management makes use of the data in their decision-making, employees will be motivated to provide the data.

I had a client where the owner did not like the e-commerce platform the company was using. He heard from someone about a stand-alone store software. I believe it was Magento if memory serves, and while it had a rich feature list and low price, I wanted to be sure all aspects and costs of this move would be considered. While the old platform was very basic, it was cloud-based and required minimal understanding to use. This platform required that it be run on managed servers and to really utilize all the flexibility there would need to be a lot of customization. Because the platform was not as simple, a store manager would need to be trained to be the person operating the store. There was also a reliance on developers to customize the platform, and of course, if there was a need for guaranteed uptime, then a service contract would be needed.

These and many more items became a part of the risk analysis. What if end users found the new platform too complicated? What if it wasn't stable enough? What if it was hard to maintain? How many extra hours would be needed to keep it operational? These and other questions fed into a risk assessment to determine the risk of the platform itself, as well as the risk of switching platforms. In the end, the owner still decided to make the move, although it would likely result in a six-figure cost to the company which would not be paid back until the third year.

However, going through the risk assessment process allowed all the principals to property identify the hidden costs, as well as really understanding the success factors that allowed making a better informed decision. Much like doing a full cost analysis and projections is important before beginning a new project, doing a risk analysis helps determine if this is the best time for the project given potential impediments and risk of failure. Even if the decision was still made to go through with the project, at least it ensured expectations were set appropriately.

25

CORPORATE FORMATION DOCUMENTS

ARE THEY IN ORDER?

*M*any businesses when they are first incorporated take the path of least resistance. Thirty years ago, that meant incorporating as a sub-chapter S corporation. This reduced double taxation and for a small business allowed simpler tax filing. Today, the most common formation is a Limited Liability Company or LLC. This has the benefits of an S-Corp but with an even simpler structure that does not require board meetings, meeting notes or bylaws. Additionally, an S-Corp is limited to 100 shareholders, and these may not be other corporations or foreign entities. For these and other reasons, LLC is the most common structure for new companies.

LLCs almost always have operating agreements which define roles, ownership, and profit allocation. I recommend reviewing these agreements annually to make adjustments based on company changes or at least to be sure there are no poor assumptions about the structure of the company. As the business grows, there may be additional sections that should be added to the operating agreement which were skipped because they were not as relevant at the formation of the company.

For example, adding a clause for sale of ownership position in case of divorce may not the first thing on founders minds, especially if all of them are single at the formation of the business. So reviewing the operating agreement with your lawyer and making changes should be a standard annual process.

The first company I founded with another partner, many years ago, is an excellent example of neglecting to think about adverse events. After spending months planning out our new business while both still working for another consulting company, we had a fleshed out business plan, new corporate branding and a sales plan. When we finally left for the new business, it felt like we did an excellent job planning. Then a non-compete lawsuit hit. My partner panicked, and unbeknownst to me, found another job - only to let me know on the day he accepted the offer. Here I was, with a new business, legal fees to deal with, and a partner that just bailed. As I check our bylaws, I realized that the only condition of a buyout of the other partner that we put in there was on the assumption of success of the business. We both assumed that if the company were not successful, there would be nothing to split as the assets would be less than liabilities and we would just shut it down. If it was successful and one of the partners left, then we would create a buyout period for the other partner. I was in a position where the company was clearly not yet profitable, but I had just invested a lot of time and money getting it started and didn't want to throw all that away to start anew. Luckily, my ex-business partner was reasonable, and we came to an agreement on the buyout which I could live with.

Having to rely on an ex-partner - or even worse on their ex-spouse to be reasonable - is a risk you should not want to take. Taking the time to put more contingency plans in place and outline the process the company will take when there are life changes for its managers or stockholders is well worth the investment of time and money in both creating and updating an operating agreement or bylaws.

Another time when it is essential to reevaluate the structure of the company prior to a company sale. While it is now common for LLCs to be sold, this was not the case with S-Corps in the past. It was considered best to change the election of the corporation to a C-Corp to make the sale possible to another company rather than an individual. Since LLCs can have corporate members, this is no longer a necessity. However, there may still be advantages in selling a C-Corp rather than an LLC. For example VCs generally only invest in C-Corps. This is an excellent time to remind you to utilize people with specialized skills, like the lawyers in a firm specializing in Mergers and Acquisitions, Accounting firms specializing in going through due diligence, and M&A consultants who can guide you through the experience with the least risk and surprises. Questions like whether to do a stock sale or an asset sale, and whether to change the corporate structure are all best answered by people with experience rather than relying on the internet.

26

PARTNERSHIP AGREEMENTS

THE RIGHT AND WRONG WAYS TO CREATE THEM

*W*hile we're on the topic of corporate paperwork, I want to provide my take on partnership agreements. There are two different types of agreements that are referred to as partnership. The first is between actual business owners or members in an LLC. The other is a contract between a service provider and the company. To some extent, I've already mentioned the owner agreement. Depending on the structure of the company they may have slightly different names, but in general, they provide a common framework for how business partners interact. I will quickly outline my preferred way to structure equity within a new company and then discuss the other kind of partnership agreements which are really service agreements.

I've been a founder or co-founder of five for-profit and several non-profit companies over my lifetime. Each time I go through the process, I try to take the lessons learned from the previous times to improve it and reduce the unexpected results. Of course, each time life has a way of throwing a wrench in the gears. But, here are some tips that come from my experience. They may work for you.

I find that everyone is quick to want to have an equal stake in a new company when founding it. I don't mean the people you hire as employees one through five, I mean the people who are equity co-founders with you. When you are planning the business, none of you have actually done anything for the company yet, so to some, it seems fair to divide full ownership by the number of people. In practice, I find this to be a mistake. People do not come with equal skills, equal time commitments, or the same financial commitments. All three would need to be balanced perfectly for the ownership to be justified as being equally split. You probably have never seen a formula for equity quite like this before, so please keep in mind this is a simplified example and is created to be the fairest equity distribution at any point in the course of the company. In practice a company would probably use a more basic method of awarding equity, this is the fairest one based on an agreement between partners which accounts for effort.

My preferred method of balancing that out is to use time and money to adjust ownership continuously. The best way to explain this is to give you an example. Keep in mind this is not the only way, but it is my favorite.

Let's say three partners are starting a business. One knows marketing, another knows technology, and the third knows operations. Each one of them can put in $5000 at the start of the business for formation expenses. One of them has a full-time job, one is retired, and the third has a limited amount of savings to live on during the startup but is not working. I will not use this for the calculation; it would merely affect total hours that each partner can commit to working on the new company and how long they can go without a paycheck or profit payout. On day one, when the papers are filed, they are each one-third partners. However, there is an immediate opportunity for the ownership to be adjusted. At the beginning of this process, all three partners should agree on the value of various work they can do for the company. For example, the tech partner may say his time is worth $200/hr while he is doing tech stuff, but $100/hr when he is doing anything else. The same $200/hr for the operations partner when he's doing operations for the company, but less when he's doing jobs that could be farmed out for less money, like making websites. The marketing guy may have a different scale, like making $1,000 per 100 people that sign up for a mailing list about the product, or $25 per sale. That is the cost of the marketing partner.

Now for sake of this example, let's assume that all partners agree on the rates of each other. Preferably, they come to that agreement before starting the company. The key to keeping feelings out of the discussion is for everyone to agree that there are jobs that could be done by others, but to save money, will be done by the partners.

Now after 3 months, we have each partner calculate their effort to date in moving the business along. For this example, let's say the tech partner has spent 100 hours in the 3 months, the operations partner spent 20 hours, and the marketing partner is still waiting for a website to be built and has not done much yet. For the sake of simplified math, we can see $200x100=$20,000 for the tech, $20x200=$4000 for the ops and $0 for the marketing partner. However, the company is almost out of cash from its initial $15,000 startup cash fund, so the marketing partner puts in another $5000. At the end of 3 months, we see the equity in the company as based on $44k total equivalent investment out of which $20k was cash, and $24k was equivalent time. The tech partner has 56.8%, the ops partner has 20.5%, and the marketing partner has 22.7%. Now, this may seem like a horrible deal for the two people who just dropped from 33%, but it's pretty equitable given the effort put forth into the company, as long as that effort is treated fairly. I would also say that in a situation like this, voting rights would still be one vote for one partner, rather than based on a percentage of ownership. In the early phase of the business, majority ownership may change frequently, and that should not be a distraction. The percentage ownership should only be used for calculating partner payouts or partner equity in case of a company sale.

Now let's jump forward nine months to the one year anniversary of the company shortly after launching the product. The tech partner has put in a total of 1200 hours, the operations partner has put in 1500 hours, with 500 of that in roles that are $100/hr, and the marketing partner has gotten 1000 people to sign up for the product and 200 people to buy the product. Let's look at the equity breakdown in this example:

1200x$200= $240,000 for the tech partner.
1000x$200 = $200,000 + 500x$100 = $250,000 for
the ops partner.
1000/100x$1000 = $10,000 + 200x$25 = $15,000 for
the marketing partner.

The breakdown of equity is now 46.6% for the tech partner, 48.6% for the ops partner, and 4.8% for the marketing partner even though he put in $10,000 cash which is as much as the other two partners combined. I used the numbers that I did because they are partly based on one of my companies, but also because I wanted non-equal ownership in the example. So in this example, it becomes clear that had the partners maintained an equal distribution, the unbilled work of two of the partners would have resulted in a much smaller equity and much smaller partner distribution for them. If one of the partners becomes a silent partner, meaning they retain ownership but do not actively work for the company, then their percentage of ownership would slowly diminish over time. If one of the partners started pulling out a salary equivalent to ½ of the rate, then only ½ of their rate would be used to calculate their additional equity. It could also be argued that two of the partners are being paid on effort and one on results. That is true, and I set it up this way on purpose for the example. You can certainly have all three being paid on effort or all three based on results.

In the final example, it has been three years since the foundation of the company. At this point the tech partner has put in a total of 5,200 hours, the ops partner 5,000 hours at full rate and 500 at a reduced rate, and the company has 100,000 people on a mailing list and has sold 25,000 products. Now in this simple example, none of the partners have taken a salary and are working purely on the profit distribution they get quarterly. In real life, there would likely be a balance between the two.

Using these numbers, we have 28% ownership for the tech partner, 28.2% for the ops partner, and 43.7% for the marketing partner. You can see the numbers have bounced around a lot. If we were to introduce salaries into the mix, that would significantly reduce the difference in equity and compensation for the partners. Also, if one of the partners became a silent partner after year 1, then their percentage of ownership would be lower each year after that.

Part of what I like in this Moving Equity arrangement is that at any point in the growth of a business the equity amount of a partner is not an arbitrary number based on initial ownership in the company prior to the success of the business, but instead is directly tied to the contribution made by the partners and in relation to contributions of the other partners. So you can see that buying out the marketing partner was much cheaper in the beginning, before he really put in much effort, and became progressively more expensive as the sales took off. Likewise, before there was much need for a CEO, the operations partner was not as busy or doing work that was at a lower rate rather than having an employee do that work, thereby saving the company money. In the example, the CTO or tech partner was front-loaded because the future growth and ability of the company rested squarely on them in the early phase of the business. For that reason, they were more heavily compensated out of profit distribution and had the company been acquired at that stage, they would receive a more significant share.

If all that is confusing, at the very least be sure that all partners have a vesting schedule that is tied to milestones. That way partners who do not hit milestones which they are responsible for, will not vest a portion of their stock, thereby reducing their shares. I could spend hours going through the pros and cons of various partnership arrangements, but let me finish with this thought. Partnerships rarely have equivalent equivalent work effort put in by each partner. So before you decide to partner with someone in a business, be sure you don't assume that the other person will always work as hard as you.

I don't want to create the impression that what I just described in a few pages is a complete architecture of an equity structure that is the most equitable, but rather to give you something to think about, even if you have a very different structure right now. It probably also makes those of you who do not have partners express a happy sigh of relief for not having to worry about such matters. I join you in that since I'm a firm believer in building companies with no partners or only silent equity partners. In my experience, having multiple active partners is, more often than not, actually detrimental to growth and often ends badly. I've helped several founders buy out their partners and increase company profitability in the process.

Af far as the other type of partnerships, for the most part, they are merely misnamed contractual vendor relationships. Most often I've seen outsourced sales relationships be called partnerships. Initially, I would try to find out where the actual joint ownership was in these deals only to discover there never was one. It just sounds better when company A is helping to sell company B's products or services to say that they have a partnership with company A and are not merely an independent reseller working on commission. Just about every time they are just that, a reseller working on a commission.

Another type of relationship I've seen when a small company provides a service to a larger one, whether it's marketing or technical, they often like to refer to that relationship as a partnership. This again is a misnomer because there is no joint ownership component. A business partnership should consist of at least two entities, whether human or corporate, who establish the third entity with mutual ownership. That would be a true partnership. Two companies who are merely collaborating on their sales efforts, or a company acting as a value-added reseller or VAR is not really a partner in the business, even if their marketing materials say, PARTNER.

SEPARATION AGREEMENTS

DON'T WAIT UNTIL YOU NEED THEM

I've already told the story of my own experience with not having a business partner separation agreement in a previous chapter. Like any legal document, the goal is to agree to terms when the relationship is good, then abide by the agreement in times of stress and change.

Besides partner separation agreements, there are also corporate separation agreements. This typically happens when a holding company sells one of its subsidiaries to another company. Usually, this happens with companies which are substantially larger than the typical company I discuss in this book, but it's still worth spending some time on this topic. Much like divorce decrees, separation agreements spell out who owns what post-separation, how the parties are to share custody of jointly utilized assets during the separation and how they will interact with each other during the separation period. These can be incredibly detailed with thousands of pages or just high-level documents with a dozen pages. The goal is the same; to provide a map for untangling parts of the business and recreating them as needed before moving on as entirely separate entities. I've been a part of two large separations over my career. One was the Ameriprise Financial separation from American Express, and the other was Marshall Field's separation from Target.

These separations involved years of time to conclude and were essentially the opposite of the actions which occur during a merger. Rather than looking for overlapping departments to consolidate, there is a need to ensure that each of the companies has departments with the staff and resources that it needs post-separation. Often, this involves keeping one department mostly intact while replicating it for the other business with predominantly new staff, location, and resources. Today, with cloud-based technology such separations are easier and faster, however no less challenging for the people involved.

Having a clear separation agreement which can be used as the basis for the separation action plan is essential for a smooth transition. As with other legal documents, the more detailed the document, the fewer surprises will pop up. The sooner the document is created, the more time there is to plan. In every case getting a business consultant with experience in managing separations will make the process much smoother and easier for the company.

28

REGULATORY/LICENSING COMPLIANCE

STAY OUT OF TROUBLE

*R*emember none of this is *legal advice*!

Licensing compliance is an area somewhere between legal compliance and contractual compliance. This is the area where you may lose your license or have to pay a fine, but likely won't end up in prison if you are found to be out of compliance. An excellent example of licensing compliance involves not using certain swear words on radio stations that operate on publicly licensed frequencies. The FCC has set up certain restrictions that it places on parties who wish to license spectrum space from the agency. While being out of compliance could lead to a loss of a license, it usually results in a fee to be paid to the FCC.

Another example may be operating a food service which is regulated by FDA standards. Being non-compliant in food storage and handling procedures may result in fines to the business, as well as a removal of the business license, effec-tively shutting the business down until the non-compliance is addressed. In any organizations dealing with regulatory compliance or licensing, knowing how well your company stands up to requirements before it is tested by the licensing body is very important. For this reason, there should be a compliance officer within the organization who works with an external auditor to validate the compliance of the organization on a regular basis, outside of official compliance check. Taking a back-burner approach to compliance could result in unplanned business disruptions, not to mention additional financial costs for the business.

If you are in an industry which does not require regulation or licensing, then congratulations you do not need to spend any part of your budget on this business expense. However do keep in mind that people who operate in industries which are regulated or licensed generally do so with less competition. So there is a trade off for the additional costs and regulation in having fewer companies competing with you.

The bottom line advice relating to operating a business which has to be compliant in its operation is to spend the money to have either an internal compliance manager or to have a compliance consultant work with your business on an annual basis to ensure that you do not risk being non-compliant and incurring the consequences. This is about limiting risk, not improving sales, but it should not be ignored.

29

CONTRACTUAL COMPLIANCE

STAY OUT OF COURT

*S*ometimes, compliance is not something mandated to maintain a license or have government agencies involved. In that case, it is most likely contractual compliance. An example of contractual compliance is being PCI DSS (Payment Card Industry Data Security Standard) compliant. See chapter 31 on PCI compliance for an example of that process.

Another example of contractual compliance may be like the one I was involved in a decade ago. A several hundred million dollar company was required to have an ISO-27001 assessment performed by its bank. This was unrelated to credit card processing, but instead was a requirement for maintaining a substantial credit line and loans. The company was in the financial space and so had higher than average risk potential. An ISO-27001 assessment measures a lot of security controls that an organization needs to have in place to mitigate data risk. Much like a PCI DSS assessment, this ISO assessment was contractually required, but it was very much in the company's interest to show low risk across the board in this assessment to maintain favorable terms.

In this instance, I helped the company prepare for the audit by running a pre-assessment to determine problem areas and suggest remediation steps to reduce risk. If this assessment was not performed, or if the company did not remediate the deficiencies then they risked losing their largest customer representing 45% of their business. Once I did the pre-audit, they realized that the remediation could take up to a year. This enabled them to negotiate additional time before the PCI audit. Had they simply gotten audited right away, they would have had much less time to implement controls to reduce risk and be in compliance, risking losing their client.. There are many different contractual compliance requirements that companies face. Having a seasoned certified auditor help them prepare for the final audit is not only acceptable, it is the best course of action!

If you find that a contractual relationship will require some form of compliance, your best course of action as the CEO is to very quickly assign a project to the appropriate department to hire a compliance specialist or ex-auditor immediately so that the company has time to find out about areas it is weak in and be able to mitigate risks well before the deadline of contract.

Of course even if you don't have a specific risk management role or department, there should be some policies dealing with risk management as well as procedures for how to act when the risk becomes reality. If you read my earlier chapter on PPS, then this should be one of the areas that is covered by all departments as part of PPS creation and management.

LEGAL COMPLIANCE

STAY OUT OF JAIL

*O*nce again, this is a reminder that there is no *legal advice* in this entire book.

Legal compliance is perhaps the most serious out of the three types of compliance. Legal compliance covers things like IRS financial compliance requirements, FTC compliance requirements, SEC compliance for financial transaction and BATF compliance for storage and transfer of munitions or alcohol. If your business has legal compliance requirements, and I could imagine very few companies that would not have some, then your compliance officer had better already have the proper processes and procedures required to be compliant. The more I worked with small businesses, the more I realized how many of these businesses are flying below the radar and hoping they are okay. There is often little proactive compliance adherence and the only efforts made to are in response to external forces, like vendors or government agencies giving notice of non-compliant status.

How can a business be sure that it is fully compliant with

all legal requirements of its operations? Well having someone who is versed in compliance come in on a consulting basis is an excellent way to minimize the costs resulting from non-compliance. There is no need to get paranoid and have a full-time lawyer on staff unless your business is sufficiently big enough to warrant it. While I probably just put myself in the crosshairs of some lawyers, I do think that compliance is more about sticking to processes and procedures and less about interpreting legal language. There is no need to reinvent the wheel in following processes that lead to full compliance, but there is a need to find someone who has already invented that wheel.

If you do email marketing, stick with companies who abide by and will flag your content if it is non-compliant with CAN-SPAM before it's sent. If you sell a digital product, work with a someone familiar with FTC regulations to be sure your sales copy and practices are well within acceptable norms. Are you on the cutting edge of blockchain software? Be sure you have someone on retainer who follows SEC and IRS opinions on digital currency so you can pivot and stay on the legal side of any regulations while your competitors drown in legal costs.

Staying compliant is all about spending a little today to minimize risk and cost tomorrow. Whether a consultant, an in-house lawyer, or a board member, someone in the company needs to focus on compliance issues and pull in legal help, when appropriate, to determine the best direction path for compliance in the company.

PCI COMPLIANCE

PAYMENT CARD INDUSTRY/CREDIT CARD PROCESSING

*T*he Payment Card Industry is primarily made up of Visa, MasterCard, Discover Card, and a handful of international card brands. The banks who issue credit cards which use the PCI brands and operate on the PCI DSS compliant networks are required by PCI to enforce specific standards on any merchants who process the cards. So, in turn, the banks require their customers to become PCI DSS compliant and to validate that they are by having a PCI QSA (Payment Card Industry Qualified Security Assessor) audit them. Audits may be required on a yearly basis, or there may be requests whenever changes to that process are made in the company. In every case, it is wise for the company to be proactive and have their PCI DSS compliance tested independently prior to the need for an official QSA tester coming in.

When I've conducted such tests for clients in the past, I've referred to them as a pre-assessment or pre-audit. The job of a PCI QSA is to test each customer as thoroughly as possible but also in the shortest amount of time as possible so they can get to their next test. The goal of a pre-assessment auditor is to conduct a more thorough test than the QSA will perform, and then propose remediation solutions for the company to address the problems with enough time for them to fix the issues. Once remediation is completed, to test again and remediate until no issues are found. Doing this will result in a smooth and fast PCI QSA assessment with the desired passing result.

Does every company need to be PCI compliant? Well, every company that accepts credit cards does indeed need to be PCI compliant. However, for companies who do not deal with credit cards directly, meaning they do not have a physical storefront and they do not have customers providing credit card information on the phone, this compliance is most likely outsourced to the cloud or web provider they use for processing credit card sales. In a situation like that, the company itself never has the credit card information; they merely have an approved code from the processor or software which indicated that the transaction went through and that the company will be receiving a deposit during the next batch cycle for the collected funds. This allows the company to minimize the need for PCI compliance of its own systems. However, removing a requirement for PCI compliance does not mean that the need for best security practices has been eliminated.

Even if credit card data is not stored on any company computers, think of all the high profile breaches in the last few years which cost companies millions of dollars and lost reputation. So be sure that everyone in customer support and other customer facing departments knows never to jot down a credit card number, or put it into a CRM, and if their calls are recorded, to let their manager know that a particular recording needs to be deleted so that credit card numbers are not stored verbally.

HIPAA COMPLIANCE

YOU MAY NEED TO COMPLY AS A VENDOR

*T*oday, companies use more outsourced services, which makes it easier to ensure compliance by transferring that responsibility and risk to a service provider. When it comes to specific regulations, like Health Insurance Portability and Accountability Act (HIPAA) compliance, much of what was once a private company HR function is now likely done by an outside provider who has to take on that compliance on behalf of the company. However, having assessed a few companies for HIPAA compliance in the last 15 years, I will say particularly when companies have not transferred that risk to an outside vendor, they are often quite severely out of compliance.

I will not mention any company names here of course. And they have all improved their stance as a result of my audits, but I will say that between PCI and HIPAA requirements about maintaining the confidentiality of Personally Identifiable Information (PII), there were often gaping process holes in these companies which represented serious security risks and needed to be closed very quickly.

Even if your company does not deal with the medical field, you may still have HIPAA obligations. For example, businesses providing services to medical companies like lawyers, accountants, and IT specialists are considered business associates who must protect the data stored by their medical clients to the same HIPAA standards as their clients. An accounting firm providing services to medical clients may need to be compliant with medical privacy requirements, even though it does not deal directly with patients' data because patient names as well as procedures performed or drugs prescribed may be on invoices sent to the patient's insurance company. Needless to say, this privacy requirement established long chains of vendors who must all be HIPAA compliance in their treatment of PII.

Find out if you have any PCI or other compliance requirements and then find out if any of your clients require you to be compliant due to their own requirements. Do this proactively and you will be in good shape!

NON-COMPETE AND NON-DISCLOSURE AGREEMENTS

HOW TO MAKE THEM ENFORCEABLE

*T*here is a lot of debate about the need for and the enforcement of non-compete agreements. There is much less controversy about non-disclosure agreements. A non-compete agreement is a contract between a company and an individual, or in some rare cases another company, restricting the non-competing party from soliciting a particular group of potential clients. Historically, this may have been as broad as a geographic restriction or a class of companies. In the last 30 years, broad restrictions on competition are routinely overturned in court, and increasingly even narrower restrictions, such as preventing a person from finding work, are thrown out. One significant exception to this is a non-compete agreement drawn up for the seller of a business upon sale. The new owners don't want previous owner to compete with the business they just purchased, so those agreements are often called golden handcuffs. The exchange of a significant amount of money for the contract to not compete for several years with the buyer is standard.

The most common type of non-compete currently in use is an active client non-compete. This agreement restricts employees from working with clients who they worked with, while at one company, when joining another company. The type of work is generally limited to the same kind of work they did for the original company, and a duration of one year or less on the restriction is the most common. So a past employee can contact and work for the same clients they worked for in the business previously, as long as it is for a type of work they did not do in the company, or if they wait out the duration and do the same kind of work. Meaning they will have full freedom to compete with their past employer on new clients who they never worked with before.

While it is very advantageous, as an employer, to try to use a contract to prevent anyone you hire from going out on their own and competing against you in the future, it is usually not worth the trouble. If you really want to have an enforceable non-compete, you have to think a bit more creatively than most companies bother to do. Think of a restriction not to compete not as something you demand from a new hire, but rather as something you buy from an existing employee. Any valid contract has to include these basic elements:

1. **Offer**: Specifies the agreed upon restriction
2. **Consideration**: What is traded for the offer
3. **Acceptance**: Both parties freely agree to terms of the contract without reservations
4. **Intention**: Creates a legal relationship, meaning the parties agree the contract should be binding and, if necessary, enforced by means of a government court.

By making sure that all these factors are present and the restriction on competing is entered into voluntarily and with a consideration other than the job itself, then this contract becomes more of a business arrangement between equals to split up clients by certain agreed-upon factors, like prior relationships. Assuming that the company does not have a monopoly on the market and that other competition exists for both entities, this should not be considered an anti-competitive act under the Sherman Act or antitrust laws. But remember I'm not giving legal advice here!

The consideration should be something other than the job. It could be monetary, or it could be a promotion, but it should be something of value and not a threat of the loss of a job. Keep in mind that your goal as an employer should not be just to safeguard your clients and keeping former employees from competing with you, but to make former employees ambassadors who tell others about how good your company is and potentially bring you new clients. You will not do that if you part on bad terms.

A contract which is accepted without reservation is one where either party may have chosen to not accept the contract without suffering greatly. A non-compete, where an employee is given no choice but to sign or be fired, is not likely to be held up in court. While there may be legal merit in the contract, the loss of job threat will be seen as duress and will likely result in a ruling for the defendant or a great reduction of scope.

The intent to create a legal relationship is a key to having the contract legally enforceable. Contracts which are not created under a jurisdiction and do not mention legal enforcement can still exist, but there is little recourse for either party if the contract is in dispute. Recently it has become more and more common to have dispute resolution through Arbitration or Mediation. These extralegal processes are generally a way to ensure faster resolution of the matter by avoiding court delays, as well as avoiding jury deliberations. Lawyers can expect to win more on technical grounds without juries, so the party that has the best contract interpretation and the best legal team is more likely to win even if common sense would show otherwise. Juries allow for more common sense and emotional arguments, which generally favors individuals over corporations. So while using Arbitration does speed things along, be sure that you are on the benefiting side of a technical argument before agreeing to use private dispute resolution methods.

Did I mention I'm not providing *legal advice*?!

NEW VENTURES

HOW TO ISOLATE THEM, AND WHY

*T*here comes a time in a business owner's life where a new opportunity strikes, which is different enough from the core business, that a decision has to be made about how best to incorporate it into the company. The right answer is often to resist the temptation to broaden the business. New ventures, new partnerships, new ways of making money are all great as they provide additional opportunities to a business owner. However, while it is tempting to use an existing team or split your marketing budget to promote the new idea inside your core business, in my experience, it is often the wrong move.

I suspect that most business leaders who do incorporate new and unproven ventures into their core businesses do it mostly out of convenience. It seems easy to redirect a portion of an existing business to focus on a new idea rather than to create a new team that does not at all rely on the old one. I have to be clear that I'm not talking about simply adding a product to a whole catalog of existing products. Instead, I'm referring to a company in a product business introducing a service business into it.

Let's use the Maytag fictional example. If you are old enough you will remember this. I will explain for the rest. Maytag had a marketing campaign based on their reputation for having excellent products. In this campaign, they had a Maytag repairman who had nothing to do all day because none of their appliances ever failed. For the sake of example, let's assume that was actually the case. Maytag had a product business and some business coach got the CEO thinking that they should have a service business as well because they are leaving all the service work to other companies; but, who would people trust more than Maytag itself to service the product. If Maytag were to move resources, spend money on advertising the new service, and change the business model to include revenue from repairing their appliances, then it would be very disappointed when it realized that none of their service people are working because their product business made such reliable appliances.

This is a fictional example of course, but Maytag in this example would have been much better served by commissioning a study, and if convinced to get into the service business, by creating a whole separate independent service company. That company could succeed or fail on its own merit with a separate P&L. The point I'm illustrating here is rather than be tempted to refocus your core business on a new idea, try to see if a new team with its own P&L could be spun up to focus on the new plan without affecting the organization working on core business.

I know a group of business partners who are very good at

testing new ideas by creating completely independent entities and making sure that a failure of one does not affect the others. However, success in one can generally be leveraged to several. The bottom line is that keeping your eggs in several baskets leads to more unbroken eggs.

35

LEGAL LIAISON

SHOULD YOU LET SOMEONE ELSE INTERFACE WITH YOUR LAWYERS?

*L*awyers cost too much anyway, why would you ever pay someone to speak with them on your behalf on top of their fees? Having done that for many years for companies, I can say that I charge much less than a law firm for my time and I only use a law firm for specific tasks requiring a legal opinion or legal interaction saving many hours of those $500/hr fees.

Much like a bookkeeper can maintain the company books, which are then checked by a CPA firm before filing, so can a legal liaison provide a similar service when dealing with contracts, negotiations, and categorizing legal issues before using a law firm for only very specific needs. The benefit for the business owner is that not only do you not have to spend time with expensive lawyers every time there are some legal issues, but that you can work with a liaison slowly over time and have them be able to explain what the needs are in legalese, minimizing lawyer billable hours and making sure they are going in the right direction from the get-go.

While I enjoy this aspect of consulting, there are relatively few people who do this. I've only met four other guys who do this type of service. But we are out there, and if you find one of us, we can save you time and money on legal matters.

I'm not going to name any past clients or provide specific details, but I have been pulled in on more than one occasion to work on pre-lawsuit contract remediation. Typically, working on making both parties happy by focusing on those items in the contract most significant to each, thus helping to put the relationship back into compliance. The lawyers are also happy to have people like me driving the negotiations and bringing them to a conclusion, rather than having unhappy clients in a stalemate.

All said and done, this is a relatively rare, specialized function that not many people perform, but it is of great benefit for any company which does not have internal legal counsel on the payroll. If you want to minimize legal expenses during contract disputes, this can save you money. If you can manage to do much of the prep work for your attorney yourself, that is the best option. If you are not well versed in legal documents, hiring a Legal Liaison may be a good way to save time and money.

36

BUSINESS SALE NEGOTIATION

HOW TO GET WHAT YOU WANT. AND THEN SOME.

*T*he key to a good company sale is preparation. The key to proper preparation is not doing it yourself! The problem for most business founders in selling their business is that they all of a sudden have two or even three jobs. First, they need to ensure that the company has their full attention and continues to grow and be profitable. Second, they need to prevent any negative rumors resulting from the business being up for sale from having an impact on sales or employee retention and performance. Third, they must go through the very grueling, detailed due diligence process. The best thing a business owner can do is keep their focus on their business and let someone else run with the business sale.

When I say business sale, I don't just mean the listing of the business. Business brokerages will sell your business to the extent of showing potential buyers any documents you have provided. Once there is serious interest in the company, the acquiring party will have a month or two to do due diligence. Brokers won't really do anything beyond forwarding the buyer requests and seller documentation back and forth during this time. If they don't have the data already from the seller, the only one who can get that data for the buyer is someone in the business, not the broker.

During that time, buyers need to confirm all their assumptions about the business, look under every rock and into every nook and cranny. It is very stressful for the buyer because often their financing to purchase the business has certain specific stipulations, and because the data they need is often not complete. It's a mad race to get as much data and to provide it to the buyer. During this time, the deal can break, or the price can change as actual data replace assumptions. If the company has good sales, the buyer will often have an incentive to speed up the deal to be able to take over and start realizing profits from those sales themselves. In a nutshell, an awful lot of stressful activity is happening, and the last thing a business owner needs is to lose track of the business focus in all the excitement.

Having a someone who does not have a job in the business, but has full access to company data to manage the "business sale process" will significantly speed up the ability to pull relevant data without bothering the owner. Having someone who is working only on your business sale, and not on any other part of your business, will ensure timely responses to your buyer prospects, streamline the process and result in the best deal for you. Remember, brokers make money by moving volume. They make more by selling several businesses, even if those deals were not the most favorable to the seller. A business sales consultant is working only on your business sale. He will be paid only based on this one deal. His interest completely parallels yours in showing the business as being worth the most and negotiating the best possible deal on your behalf.

The last time I acted in this capacity, I can say it was an awful lot of work. I earned my commission over the course of several grueling and stressful months while enabling the owner of the business to focus on running the business and maintaining sales. Because I understood the owner's priorities and hard NOs, I was able to negotiate away things he cared little about to be sure he got the things he did care about. I also believe that because the buyers did not use a business buying consultant, they were vulnerable to emotional decision making. In effect, they were, selling themselves emotionally rather than being removed from the deal to minimize any emotional decision making.

RESTRUCTURING TO FACILITATE A COMPANY SALE

HOW TO MAKE YOUR COMPANY MORE ATTRACTIVE

With no immediate plans to sell the company, there is usually a balance between re-investment for growth and taking increased profits by stockholders. In the early stages,, that balance is often more skewed toward reinvesting for growth, and more toward extracting profits later in a company's life.

If the goal is to make the company attractive for an acquisition, there are specific changes in operations, finance, and structure which can positively affect the price of a business. First, while you can not change the past, you can still reframe it. If there are reasonable explanations for certain past decisions which can be explained to be intended for future profitability, then those decisions should absolutely be reframed in that way, even if the original reasons may have been different.

You can also change things the company is doing today, so look at the company from the perspective of a buyer. There are just a few reasons buyers purchase companies:

- The company may have some technology or patent that the buyer wants.
- The company has employees that the buyer wants.
- The company has customers that the buyer wants to sell additional products.
- The company will create a good return on investment (either through selling the company again or by generating income from profits) for the buyer after some tweaks.

While the first several are generally cases of mega-companies buying small companies for some specific reason, it represents a small percentage of acquisitions each year. The last reason is the most common reason that a buyer is interested in buying a company. Generally, they are looking for companies which will pay back the purchase price in the least number of years before generating additional profit. Ideally, buyers look for companies which can return the purchase price in less than 24 months of sales.

The buyer may make major changes to the company to accomplish a fast return, or they may simply leave everything as is and wait for a return. In every case, the more profit a company makes compared to its asking price, the more attractive it is to a buyer. For most business acquisitions, the standard measurement used to compare companies for the buyer is EBITDA and it stands for:

Earnings Before Interest, Taxes, Depreciation and Amortization. **EBITDA** *= Net Profit + Interest +Taxes + Depreciation + Amortization.*

It is a good metric of profitability for a company, but does not take into account cash flow, which is, of course, another important measurement when buying a business. It also does not highlight the potential expense of replacing old equipment, which might be high in some companies.

There are ways to restructure the company to increase the EBITDA, at the expense of cash flow, to make the company more appealing. There are also ways to change the profit per employee ratio of the business by using contractors. Conversely, if the goal is to reduce external dependencies, which some buyers dislike, it is possible to restructure to a more internal weighted cost structure by bringing on new hires. Keep in mind, the snapshot of the company as it exists during the sale will be assumed to have been the case in the past by the buyer, at least until they do due diligence. This allows you the flexibility to restructure a company just months prior to listing it for sale. Of course, there should not be any deliberate deception to the prospective buyers. Merely, much as repainting the house before putting it up for sale will make the buyer see the new clean version of the house, changes made to the structure of the company can make it more appealing and result in more interest and perceived value from potential buyers. This way, you may tweak your current EBITDA to be more favorable for acquisition and get past buyer filters that you would otherwise not.

Another helpful thing to keep in mind is that the buyer will be looking at your P&L for the previous year and the last several full quarters of the current year. So if you can get to a Letter of Intent before a quarter closes accounts, you will not have to rush and provide the reconciled financials that include that quarter. In practical terms, getting an LOI in March, June, September or December means your current quarter will not be expected to provide audited financials for the current quarter. Of course, if the current quarter is showing significant growth, you probably want to delay getting the LOI until you know you can include that quarterly result in the due diligence that starts with the LOI.

Whatever the reason your company is for sale, it will be in your best interest to show the buyer that their investment will be recouped quickly. Naturally, as you get closer to selling the business, it is time to stop all long-term and most short-term re-investing and cash out your profit. If you can sell inventory at above wholesale costs, you should do so since you will likely receive only discounted value of any inventory transferred during the sale. If you can receive any discounts for terminating contracts, you should do so before you sell the business. If you can stop your advertising spend or at least significantly reduce it without killing all sales, then do that as well. Why spend money helping the new owner get clients after you sell the company if you won't be compensated for that expense post-sale? Essentially, take whatever you can comfortably take out of the business without appreciably reducing its value. Conversely, if you can extend a lease for your office space in exchange for a couple of free months right now, then do that. The offer on your business will not likely be affected by the lease contracts on office space, furniture, or other ordinary long-term expenses.

The best way to make sure that you take as much as you can out of the business pre-sale is to work with a business sales consultant who has helped businesses get sold in the past. Remember this is not a business broker who makes their money by getting as many deals closed per month as possible. This is more like a wedding planner who works on your behalf making sure you are happy on the day you sell your business.

38

PREPARATION FOR DUE DILIGENCE

IN ANTICIPATION OF SELLING THE COMPANY

*O*nce you have decided to sell your business, it is time to make sure that all the T's are crossed and the I's are dotted. Be sure that you have three years of audited financial records and that all accounts are reconciled. If being purchased by a private company or individual, then you may be able to negotiate lesser requirements, but remember, any time you negotiate down conditions you are also negotiating down the potential sale price. Compile any documented liabilities arising from past sales by company customers. Any liabilities related to warranties or future deliverables should be calculated. Compile all contracts currently in effect as well as contracts for the last 12 months even if no longer active. The buyers will likely make that part of their DD effort and anything not provided will affect their offer. All IT related information, all HR information, and all governance documents should be put together into a virtual Document Vault. This can be a Dropbox folder or some other means of gathering, organizing and sharing documents, as long as it will be a single shared set of documents to ensure that everything is accurate and indisputable for the company sales contract.

Surprises kill deals - the last thing a seller needs is a surprise about the buyer's ability to deliver. Likewise, the last thing the buyer needs is a seller who keeps changing their mind about their obligations or history. Putting all the information which will be required by the likely buyer together before it is requested will ensure a smooth sale in the shortest amount of time. The more you can demonstrate being prepared and organized, the more convinced the buyer will be that you ran your business soundly. Of course if you have already invested time into building out your PPS, as I previously described, then you can leverage the operational maturity of your company for a faster due diligence process. That translates to getting the highest price for your business with the least amount of negotiation.

The typical Due Diligence process happens after a buyer has determined that they are interested in your company and you have spent some time negotiating a price range. I say range because items discovered during the DD period may adjust the price up or down. Once you get the Letter of Intent (LOI), the buyer will be digging through your company more thoroughly than an IRS agent. Meanwhile, you are usually prohibited from soliciting any more offers for the company during their DD period. If you genuinely have multiple interested buyers, do not commit to one too early. Let them both kick the tires while you continue to collect the profit from your business. Take the money you would have reinvested in the business and consider it your extra payment for going through DD.

While the buyer may ask for 60 or even 90 days of DD, it is something that can be negotiated. Generally the shorter a DD period, the better it is for the seller. If the buyer ends up lowballing you after DD due to something they didn't like, then the sooner you can entertain other buyers the better. If they have no problems during the DD and are ready to move forward, the sooner you do the deal, the sooner you get paid. Your goal should be a 30 day DD if at all possible and 45 days if there is no way to do 30. If you make the buyer realize that there is money coming into the business that you will be keeping rather than reinvesting during the DD, they are more likely to agree to a shorter period. Also, keep in mind that you can still decide to back out of the deal if you discover something smells funny during the DD on the buyer's side. For instance, if the buyer is financing the transaction through an investment bank or private equity which will subordinate your ongoing payments, that may put your ability to collect the full sale value at risk. You may want to back out or front load payments in that situation. You also should consider the time that DD is being performed on your business as the perfect time to investigate the buyer as well.

Unless this is a highly unusual all-cash deal, odds are you will not receive the majority of the purchase price until later - possibly several years later. You may also receive a smaller earn out if the business you sold underperforms, if the purchase agreement has such a stipulation. Since you will no longer be making executive business decisions, you are at the mercy of the buyer to run the business well, hence the need for outstanding legal help in crafting business sale agreements.

This is not the time to skimp on a lawyer. Plan on spending one percent of the purchase price on legal bills. Five to ten percent on a broker. Eight to ten percent on a business sales consultant, and of course additional expenses on financial auditors. Some of these expenses will happen even if the deal does not go through, so be sure you have some money set aside to cover unexpected expenses if the business does not sell or if you are forced to go through this process with multiple buyer prospects.

While we're on this topic, be aware that your cash payment will most likely be 25-30% of the overall deal. It may be in cash, which is almost always preferable, or some part may be in stock. If you have high confidence in the buyer, a stock portion has the opportunity to be worth more over time than cash. However, you are always assuming more risk with a stock deal, as well as having restrictions on when you can convert stock to cash. The next 50-60% will likely be structured earn-out based on the newly acquired company hitting some milestone. The risk for you, of course, is that you have a much-reduced role or possibly no role in the company, so it is really up to the buyer to guide the combined companies to hit those goals. It is best not to count your cash here - at least not at top value. Assume that the company will not hit its targets. Will you still be happy with the deal if you end up getting 70% or even less of the amount of sale price?

Finally, there is usually a final cash payment. This is the big reward at the end of the deal. Ensure in your sales contract that any money paid to you after the initial date of sale accrues interest. After all, delayed payment by the buyer means that the cost of capital is cheaper for them. You, not they, should be profiting from what is essentially a loan to them for the purchase of the business. Remembering to add 6% interest could make a million dollar difference over the course of 4-year payout.

39

REFERENCE CHECKS

HOW TO MAKE SURE THEY'RE REALLY HAPPENING

here is one other area related to hiring which I did not mention in earlier chapters. Reference checks and background checks have been around as a best practice for business for centuries, but in the age of instant information, fewer and fewer companies seem actually to be doing them. Almost every company I have consulted with has done a poor job of vetting their prospective new hires. At best, the company will do a criminal background check only on employees hired in the accounting department. At worst they do no background checks at all. Combine this with a general lack of verifying references and what you end up with are blind hires.

Most companies are hiring people solely on how well they presented themselves during an interview or two. This is great for extroverts who are very good at talking about their past success, but bad for introverts who may have been responsible for the success of that extrovert. Of course, it's not just a matter of introverts vs. extroverts. Many people learn how to present their best side at an interview and minimize their potential problems. Without checking references and also doing background checks, a company risks hiring someone who has a history that shows them differently than the way they present themselves in an interview.

While a credit check may not be necessary for all new hires, a criminal check absolutely should be. The point here is to go into a business relationship with eyes wide open. A company may decide to hire someone with a prior criminal conviction because it was many years ago, or because it was for an issue where laws have not caught up to public opinions, but either way, it is best that the company is aware of any history. A credit check generally shows a person's ability to live within their means and budget appropriately. Of course, there are unexpected bumps in life that may affect someone's credit usage.

I can say that when I got divorced, my credit usage absolutely went up as I was recovering from that event. More recently I was a co-founder of hardware company building a product for podcasting. During this time I had only a few client projects as most of my energy was focused on the startup. In the end, the startup floundered when we lost our chief engineer, and the product never got released. As a result, I had much higher usage of my credit cards because I had been using credit during the 18-month startup in anticipation of being able to pay them off after our product launch. I may not be any less creditworthy as a result of this in my own mind, but as far as a credit report would show, I had much more outstanding debt, and so I probably showed up as a higher risk during that time.

When it comes to reference checks, the best answers are going to be from the last immediate supervisor for that employee. It is understandable that many people do not want to have their boss know they are looking for other work, so what I suggest is to speak with other references the person provided, but make any job offer contingent on a final reference check with their boss. This way you can make an informed decision based on the latest facts. While this may cause a prospect to be nervous, it really should not. I tell these prospective new hires that the only information I will be verifying after they give their notice at the old job is the following:

- The last salary paid
- Hire date and title
- Promotion history
- Training history

All of these questions are fact-based, and you should have no issues getting straight answers. You should already have all of these answers directly from the candidate, so you are merely verifying if their responses correspond to what their supervisor says. Keeping the questions relevant to their job and fact-based is essential. While you may ask questions which are open-ended, a good manager will refrain from answering any questions which do not have specific fact answers as it may lead to a complaint with the EEOC. For that matter asking a question which may show a bias based on the eighth discrimination types recognized by the EEOC could also lead to problems.

If you are selling products to kids, check that your new hire is not a registered pedophile. If you are hiring an accounting person, be sure they don't have a conviction for financial fraud. Use common sense.

Ultimately, all you should care about is truth in advertising. If a candidate said they did something, did they actually do it or simply take credit for it.

One last note about drug testing: Many companies require drug testing due to contract requirements of their vendors such as military contracts, liability insurance contracts or financial service contracts. As a consultant, I have been required multiple times to take drug tests before starting a project at a company. Keep in mind that unless you have an external requirement to test employees, it may only make sense for jobs where physical safety is critical, like driving a forklift. Drug tests often show false positives and false negatives. So any time a test comes back positive for some substance, its routine to schedule a retest right away. I had one test come back positive shortly after eating several poppy seed bagels that day. Thankfully retaking the test the next day showed a different result.

When it comes to jobs requiring operation of company vehicles or dangerous equipment, regular and random drug and alcohol screening are more useful than a single drug test at hire. For that matter, regardless of your opinion of drugs, letting a prospect know that your company does random drug tests for specific jobs will likely make someone who uses recreational drugs much less interested in the position.

IV

BEFORE THE SALE

PRODUCT LINE EVALUATION

HOW DO WE STACK UP AGAINST OUR COMPETITORS?

*D*on't trust anyone who actually sells a product to accurately evaluate how their own product stacks up against the competition. Companies create product comparisons which are designed to highlight benefits of their own products while ignoring strengths of competing products. Likewise, a jaded employee who is dissatisfied with the company she works for will never give you an unbiased opinion about the company's offerings and those of competitors. So who should you trust to do market research? And what type of research should you do? Keep in mind, we are talking about actual competitive analysis, not marketing, which shows a chart where your product has all the features, and the competition has very few. That is stacking the deck for marketing and tells you nothing about your actual competition.

There is a market preference, there are feature comparisons, and there is a competitive advantage. Each of these measurements may show a different winner. So how do you really know how well your product or service stand up to competition? You need someone who is unbiased about your products to look at all of these measurements and provide you with a breakdown of each which can be used for product planning as well as marketing strategy.

Let's look at the easiest one first: Feature comparisons on websites are usually paid for by the marketing departments of whichever products seems to come out on top in the comparison. That is because they start with the end in mind and only then create a feature comparison that highlights their strengths while minimizing weaknesses. This type of comparison is not useful for business. To create a comparison that can be used for strategic planning, product redesign and to increase your competitive advantage, an accurate, unbiased comparison must be made. This would include the purchase and evaluation of your and competitive products or services by an independent party. The consultant would evaluate all the features, ease of use, time to execute, support offered and other facets of the product. Once complete, a chart illustrating where your product stands will provide a snapshot of the competitive plane. It may well be the case that the lack of some features is by design or prioritization and the result of business decisions, not merely omission - for example, to reduce cost, reduce size or improve efficiency. The goal of this exercise is to be keenly aware of where the company product stands compared to competing products. There may well be good reasons for the lack of some features, but if there is not a good reason, this exercise helps to uncover what is missing and where the next iteration of the product needs to go. As a side note, if you are interested in how products are invented and innovated, google TRIZ which is a theory of iterative invention-related tasks.

If we look at market preference, we are looking at sales data or at least estimates. Using measurements of mentions of products online and reading reviews of products can help determine a market snapshot. Here the specific advantages and disadvantages of a product are not significant. Instead, it is more about a feeling of preference in online and traditional media including videos. The perception may be based on false ideas, but it does illustrate what consumers will likely see when they are interested in similar products. Market preference may be driven by brand preference, where consumers simply like one brand over another in the absence of any real distinction. Or it may be based on factors completely unrelated to the brand or the product which are currently dominating news cycles. Knowing this can help a company adjust the marketing message to counter negative preference and build a positive one. Linking your product to events can backfire, as seen in a Pepsi commercial with Kendall Jenner. It was the most disliked ad in history shortly after it was aired. The formulation or taste of Pepsi didn't change, but the association did change and was reflected in lower projected sales estimates.

Competitive advantage is not always apparent, and often it is not felt until it is too late to compete successfully. For instance, Costco has a competitive advantage over most other stores that carry similar products. Because Costco makes the majority of its profit from the yearly membership fees that it charges, it is free to reduce the prices of its product below levels which competitors can offer. Additionally, Costco sells products only in large volume, so it takes advantage of volume discounts when purchasing. Costco has done a great job of marketing using its competitive position, first by targeting small businesses and offering discounted prices on thousands of bulk items, then by advertising to families with promises of the same wholesale prices that companies pay. I remember seeing the first wholesale club in the 80s, and while it looked then much like Costco does today, it could not offer prices like Costco because they had just one club worth of purchasing volume. Over the years Costco and its only real competitor, Sam's Club, have gobbled up or displaced all other wholesale clubs through their ability to buy in more massive quantities. Knowing where a company in your market segment has a competitive advantage allows better planning and differentiation to avoid being displaced.

Of course, if your goal is to be acquired, knowing how to make it more attractive to acquire you rather than compete with you is the difference between a payday and a bankruptcy.

PRODUCT VIABILITY STUDY

SHOULD WE ADD THIS TO WHAT WE DO?

*P*roducts can be physical, virtual, interactive, electronic, or dozens of other categories. But one thing that is true for all of them is that a company should only invest the time and money into developing a product if there is a reasonable demand for that product. Of course, there is always some risk, and bringing a new product to market cannot be done without any risk. But doing a product viability study will help determine whether the product is likely to be wanted and therefore purchased by consumers as well as whether the product can be reasonably produced and deployed to market. If either side of the equation is off, the risk of moving forward with creating the product is substantially increased.

A product viability study should start off with market evaluation, competitive landscape study and identifying your target customer. The next items to research are on the cost side of the product. What is the R&D cost? Are there additional startup costs? What are the additional labor costs?

GENE NAFTULYEV

What are other ongoing costs? What is the opportunity cost? Only after knowing both sides of the equation is it possible to determine whether this product is worth bringing to market. There is no such thing as a product worth bringing to market at any cost, nor is there a product so good that it can't fail. Plenty of companies have staked their reputations on these two extremes and paid a large price as a result.

Right now, we all have smartphones with a myriad of tools including a talking personal assistant. Almost 25 years ago, Apple introduced the Newton, the first personal digital assistant. While some would argue that the Newton was the ancestor to the iPhone, Steve Jobs has vehemently disagreed with that point. The Newton was a new class of device that addressed a need that people didn't realize they had, with hardware that was both too expensive and from my recollection, too clunky for anyone other than true enthusiasts to really use. This product should have never been green-lit after a viability study. Apple was unable to produce a small enough product with enough features to make anything more than a novelty product that only nerds bought.

Yes, I admit I owned a Newton in 1994. Beyond the novelty aspect, there was little practical use. I remember writing directions down on a Newton during a trip, only to have the batteries die during my drive resulting in a search for a gas station so I could buy new AA batteries to power it on and get my directions. Apple spent a lot of money researching and developing this product for four years. I suspect they released it merely because so much money had already been spent on it that they didn't want to cancel the project.

Eventually, the product was scrapped when Steve Jobs

came back to Apple. Jobs had the ability to do a product viability analysis in his head in a way that almost no one else can. He had guided Apple to so many revolutionary products, not because he took random chances, but because he innately understood that products should address the needs of people, even if the people do not yet know they have those needs, and do it in a way that makes Apple a very nice profit.

Steve Jobs understood this principle better than anyone. But you don't need a Steve Jobs in your company if you simply perform a Product Viability Study before spending money rolling out a new product.

PROTOTYPE OUTSOURCING

WHO CAN MAKE THE FIRST ONE FOR US?

*I*f your company is looking at creating a new product one of the first questions after how big is the market, should be:Who will make the prototype? If you are simply modifying an existing product that your company is already manufacturing, then you may have this capability covered internally. You probably have a product development lab that can create prototypes. However, if you are a reseller, a new company, or a company wanting to make a product that is different than anything else you currently sell, you may not have that capability.

If you've never looked into it, finding a prototype outsourcer may seem like a daunting task. But way before getting to a physical prototype, you should be sure that you go through concept validation. Make sure that the idea of what you want the product to be is clear and the concept can be described in a way that typical buyers can understand. Once the concept is validated, more than likely you will need to create a digital version of your product. I don't mean a digital one you can sell, rather a 3D mockup of what it will look like, preferably with the ability to manipulate it in 3D. This phase is called wire-framing. If you are going to be doing crowd-funding for your product be sure to capture every iteration of work starting with the wireframe to show off in your marketing upon launch.

Once you've further validated the product with the wire-frame 3D mockup and are sure that the idea deserves to move on to the next step, get ready for your first physical prototype. If the product is purely physical, you will likely need CAD software to build the model of your product that CNC machines or 3D printers are capable of creating. While CAD software can be used to create 3D mockups, it is not true that all 3D mockup software can create CAD/CAM files. So if you used software not designed for generating CAM files, the files used by machines to actually make a physical object, then you will need to have someone re-create your 3D mockup in a CAD/CAM software. Once that is done, you will be able to get physical mockups of your product. If the product is a physical item, then the mockup will be very close to the final product. An example of a physical product I was involved with is the DecadentMinimalist.com wallet (*Use discount code GENE when ordering*).

Of course, if your product is more complicated, like the failed electronic audio product I was an involved with, then you are only part of the way there. Once the physical elements of the product were prototyped, there was still an electronics component which involved making a small batch of custom boards with all the chips on them. This process is more complicated than the CAD/CAM portion since you both have to have a custom board prototyped, but also that board will be running some software, which needs to be written by a developer and debugged before it can be loaded onto the prototype system. For the PodcasterPro™ product that we created, this process took a long time. The design phase was probably four months, the software functionality was eight months, physical prototype CAD was two months, and board prototype was about four months. All these had to be completed before the first operational prototype was finished. Of course, while this was going on, there was marketing and PR activity, promotional deals, and of course trying to operate the business as lean as possible.

For another product I worked on, a yoga mat, prototyping was predominantly finding a material that was close to the mat as possible, but which was intended for a different purpose. Sometimes if you are lucky, you can simply adapt a completely different product as a usable prototype allowing you to get through prototyping while having spent much less money.

The key here is to have as much information about the product to be prototyped as possible before you meet with a prototyping shop. The more details you have, the lower their price will be because fewer assumptions need to be made. Based on my experience, always assume it will take twice as long to do the prototype as you are initially quoted. Any time something has to be created from scratch, the pessimistic time estimate is probably the correct one.

PRODUCT DEVELOPMENT
CONSULTATION

STEPS TO BRING IT TO MARKET!

A Product Development Consultant is someone who is effectively a producer for a product. This role could include a Product Manager, as well as many previous roles mentioned above. A product development consultant helps the company work through the process of developing or deciding to acquire new products. Some of these required skills are based on an ability to build the product. While this person will not actually be making the prototype or product, they should know how similar products are made, the timelines for building your type of products and what costs should be calculated for the new product. On the flip side, they need to understand your buyers, the needs which are not being met and how a new product could fit into the company product ecosystem. Companies which come out with products on a regular basis will likely want to have an in-house Product Development Manager who may then have a Product Development team. For smaller companies or companies which do not often develop new products, it is better to go with an external resource who works with multiple companies and can bring expertise from having gone through the product development process many times.

I hope it is becoming apparent that developing one successful product is hard enough. Adding additional products which are successful takes a lot of effort and often can not be done quickly. The rush to a new product can be seen in many "failures to launch" from both small and large businesses. We have examples of failed, often very expensive, product launches in products like New Coke, Microsoft Bob, the aforementioned Apple Newton, Microsoft Zune, and the Netflix spinoff Quickster which cost the company millions before they changed course. All these products had fatal flaws that should have been spotted before launch. Unfortunately, sometimes the desire to get something launched outweighs the risk of doing that.

You can not eliminate all risks when developing a new product, but making sound business decisions based on as much insight as possible is much easier when you have someone with previous experience taking the lead on creating your next great product. Finding a good product development consultant may take a while, so if you want help developing a new product, plan to start the search several months earlier.

44

PRODUCT ACQUISITION NEGOTIATION

WHY CREATE IT WHEN WE CAN JUST BUY IT?

I'm a big fan of Shark Tank the TV show. Well, maybe not a superfan since I don't watch it every week, but I do binge watch it in bursts on Hulu. Like any reality show, there are exaggerated moments of tension and drama. But if you look past that, there are frequently outstanding lessons for entrepreneurs. My favorite shark is Kevin O'Leary, which might come as no surprise to you by this chapter of the book. I don't know if Kevin uttered the subtitle of this chapter on one of the episodes or if he only did that in my imagination, but it sure sounded like him in my head. Product acquisition is a much faster, albeit potentially costly method of getting a product to market. Acquisition can take the form of a business purchase, a licensing deal or a wholesale purchase agreement.

Many companies have made the mistake of thinking that doing the production of a product in-house is a way to save money. There may be plenty of reasons why in-house production is beneficial, like putting "Made in USA" on the product, but very rarely is it cheaper than using a manufacturer who specializes in that kind of product. Companies, and departments for that matter, are most effective when they execute tasks that they know the best. If your business knows how to sell a product you currently manufacture, it may be cheaper for you to outsource the manufacturing of another product that you can add to your catalog. For that matter, it is often good to evaluate the benefits of outsourcing your current product production. While I do not think that everything needs to be made in China, I'm also not a big fan of inefficient in-house production.

Apple, as usual, is the exception, but then again, they have a UFO as their headquarters, and I'm pretty sure there are pet unicorns at Apple for employees to ride. Try to be like Apple or Amazon, but realize that you are not yet them and what works for them may not work for you. For companies like Apple, it's often preferable to buy small companies that make the parts they want to use in their products rather than creating those parts from scratch in-house. But remember, even Apple is using companies like Samsung to produce some elements that go into the iPhone. The idea that somehow products that are made in-house are inherently better is an anachronism from a time when Asia was the super cheap producer of substandard products. The reality is, most expensive and even luxury products for sale right now are at least partly made outside the US. You can just as easily make either a good product or inferior quality product in the US. I'm not speaking about the design, but only about the manufacturing aspects here. Manufacturing in the US is the same as overseas, whether it's China, Taiwan, or the Philippines. The quality of the production has more to do with the adherence to quality controls like ISO 9001, Kaizen, or Six Sigma than it does with the nationality of the staff. A certified company overseas will likely produce a superior product compared to a US company which produces the same product but has no certifications or quality management.

Good quality always costs more, but in some countries, the cost of good quality is less than the price of poor quality manufactured in-house. Do not assume that local manufacturing is always better. Having said that, do not expect that the cost of US production will necessarily be much more expensive for every type of product. Some products can undoubtedly be produced in the US for the same or similar costs In those instances, it may be worthwhile to do just that.

When you find a product that can enhance one of your products, then absolutely look at product acquisition costs as that may be cheaper and faster than replicating your own version of the product. For that matter, if you find a product that is absolutely right for your company and you want to be sure others are not able to sell it, find out the cost of an exclusive license for the product from the patent holder and get the ability to sell it with no competition.

Remember, you need not be the company that invented a product to become the sole distributor of that product. And the corollary is that you don't need to manufacture and sell a product if licensing it to someone else generates sufficient income for you.

45

MANUFACTURING IN CHINA

IS IT RIGHT OR WRONG FOR US?

*C*hinese manufacturing has gotten a bad reputation for some good reasons and some stereotyping. The thing that Chinese manufacturers seem to have in common, which is different from other countries, is that they place a significant value on time. More often than not, to them, it is better to manufacture a product faster, even if it has some defects, and just fix things in the next version. Most other manufacturing countries have more of a measure twice and cut once culture. Meaning they would instead not start the production line unless everything is perfect. I think that is part of the reason that Chinese manufacturing is often seen as poor quality. But it is important to note that it doesn't have to be poor quality, nor does it always end up being cheap.

Part of the reason for the lower prices in Chinese manufacturing has to do with the much cheaper labor costs. While 2017 costs are around $3.60 per hour, historically Chinese labor costs have been much lower, often under $1 per hour. The other reason manufacturing is cheaper in China is due to the proximity of raw materials. China not only has a large labor force, but they also have many mineral processing in their country. Only Russia and the US have more abundance in natural mineral resources than China. China is now also a leader in mining resources in Africa, so Chinese companies have advantages that many other manufacturers do not. All these lower costs end up creating a supply chain that can often be significantly cheaper for Chinese companies.

With a large pool of manufacturing companies in China, you may be able to find an existing product that is similar in design and can address your needs. You can save a lot of time by getting a white label version of this product, with your custom branding on it. In fact, you can often get product ideas by browsing Alibaba or some of the other Chinese product catalog sites. Due to the variety of production facilities and the low cost of entry, China really opens up the possibility of manufacturing to even small companies.

But China is not all wine and roses. There are issues that just about every company I've worked with have seen along the way. The most common is probably missing delivery deadlines. Most shipping from China is coming in containers on ships because only very light products can be shipped by air economically. This slow shipping creates a much longer turnaround period compared to local manufacturing. On top of the long shipping times, unpredictable delays and costs can come out of the customs clearance process. Finally, to add more delay potential, China has many more holidays and longer than the US. For many US customers, the surprise of a factory shut down for a week or month due to some holiday in China can lead to missed deadlines. Do not expect anything that is coming out of China to hit specific delivery dates. Treat all dates as a best-case scenario and be pleasantly surprised if you actually get things on time.

Another common issue with China is minimum acceptable quality. Every company has a certain expectation of the quality of their products. It is different for everyone, but since Chinese manufacturers work with so many different clients, they tend to let the client drive how high the level of quality needs to be rather than being proactive. To many American eyes, Chinese samples seem to always come in at a high quality, but the first production run is often at a lower quality. The Chinese company is putting its best foot forward and showing this is what we are capable of doing while the American company sees that as the minimal quality they will get. To the Chinese company, any sample is just that, an example of capabilities and the conversation about quality deviation from that sample has not taken place yet. Americans, on the other hand, are always surprised that someone would deliver products in worse shape than samples. The issue is communication and not making assumptions. Of course if PPS is enforced in the manufacturing company with a certification like ISO 9001, then it is much more likely every sample will be identical.

Successful companies that do business in China know that they need a man on the ground. Whether a local who works for the buyer or someone flying in to spend time with the contract manufacturer, it is vital to have that on-site access. Given the delays in shipments already mentioned, having someone who can make real-time corrections will significantly speed up all manufacturing and reduce errors. Additionally having someone on-site allows for more comparison shopping of factories or wholesalers in China in a way that merely looking online will not.

Finding the right resource to help a company become familiar with manufacturing in China will be the difference between a successful offshore product production and failed product launches.

46

PRODUCT PHOTOGRAPHY

LOOKING GOOD!

*N*ot every company has physical products, so not every company will need product photography. But if you have physical products, having a variety of great photos will help ensure that people buying your products, whether on Amazon or your website, will be able to get a good feel for the quality and finish of the products. Product photography is often neglected by small businesses who place spending money on a professional photographer low on their priorities list. However it doesn't have to be expensive or complicated, so there is no excuse for bad product photos.

The biggest misconception in what a photography customer is paying for is not all the professional equipment a photographer has, but rather it is the time that she has put in behind the lens which enables that photographer to very quickly compose the most attractive shots of the subject. So while professional photographers do generally have top-notch equipment worth tens of thousands of dollars, it is mostly their experience that you should be concerned about.

If I hire a professional photographer I will be most interested in how long have they been doing it professionally and, of course, examples of similar products they have shot to be sure they can do my product justice. Whether they are located in a swanky downtown office or a warehouse neighborhood does not play at all into my consideration.

When you do hire a professional photographer these days, it is also common for them to either offer video or to work with a videographer who can do that service. Product photos are a requirement; product videos are a differentiator. If a similar product only has pictures and you have video, the odds of you winning that sale just went up. A product video is even useful for digital products as it can show screen capture, talking heads, and animation to convey the message in a way that photographs can not. While we have only focused on (ha!) sales photos and video up to now, there is an even more significant need for customers to be able to see pictures and videos as part of a help and support system for your products post-purchase. Consider using the same professional quality photo or video company for support and training videos as you use for your sales material. Your customers will appreciate a seamless look, and it may benefit you by getting lower pricing from the photographer.

Up to now, I've focused on products as either physical or digital. If you have a service company, you are in no less need of photos and video. Your service delivery people are your product, and your potential customers want to see them. I'm a big believer in using actual employee images for many reasons. Using stock images of beautiful models may look nice, but most people instinctively know that your company staff are not likely all models. So they question: Why do you not present your actual employees in these images? Is there something you are hiding? The first company I am aware of who started using employee photos for selling physical products was MacWarehouse in 1992. They started putting photos of call center people on the top corners of their printed catalog. Initially, it was one employee, then as they found customers calling and asking for that one person, they realized that people like to see who they are actually talking to and they put a different person on every page. This was a great marketing win for them. Of course, that was in the days when phone support and sales were all based in the US.

The Roy H. Williams Agency used actual employees in many Morris-Jenkins TV ads. This helped make the company the most popular HVAC company in the state. Selling a service company with photos and video is no different than selling products from a product company.

The bottom line is, do not neglect the quality of the image you present to the world. Hire a professional photographer for products and staff photos and use video to show potential customers what it looks like to work with you.

47

PUBLIC RELATIONS

HOW TO GET THE ATTENTION OF
THE PRESS

*T*wenty years ago, if you wanted to get noticed by the media, you had to hire a Public Relations (PR) firm for months, if not years, to give them time to get publicity about your business or products. Luckily the internet changed that and now social media may actually get you much more attention than traditional media. There is little difference regarding impact whether people see comments about your business from a friend on Facebook or in an ad you purchased on Facebook. In fact, traditional media is now forced to spend their money advertising on Facebook or risk losing their audience. While Facebook and Google do not want to be seen as media companies, they are essentially the new media companies.

Major media in specific niches may still hold an essential place for promoting your products. If your company is making parts for airplanes, getting trade publications to talk about your latest products is very beneficial, but since social media like Facebook and LinkedIn know where their members work, you could also directly target people who fit the profile of your customers there. You may also join affinity groups or special interest groups on social media and then freely post news directly where people in that industry hang out, as long as it does not get too "salesy." Of course, doing this will require that someone in the company is responsible for all this social content.

Does that mean there is no longer a place for PR? Not exactly. There is very much a place for PR for targeted product launches, book launches, or other newsworthy events. The real questions are: Do you have someone in your marketing team that can do the legwork of contacting both traditional and online media and keeping them in the loop about your story? Or do you simply want to hire a PR firm to do the distribution for you? If you're going to have an employee handle traditional media, services like HARO - Help a Reporter Out - or BusinessWire are all ways to connect with conventional as well as online media.

The key to making PR a good bang for the buck is to do as much as possible for free, then carefully select territories and segments of media where you want your PR to be focused before you hire an agency or use a service like PR Newswire. Conversely, you could hire a marketing agency who also does PR and let them handle both your paid advertising and native advertising like product reviews or mentions in media.

The democratization that the internet brought to advertising has also muddled the distinction between paying for a PR service which gets you articles written by the press and articles in the media which are fully paid for known as native advertising. Either way, you are paying to show up in news stories, but who you pay has somewhat changed.

What has not changed is that sending product samples to people who run websites or writers for publications can still get you mentioned with no cost beyond the price of the sample. During several product launches that I was involved with, we were able to get mentioned in the press for minimal cost by merely reaching out to specific journalists and websites, providing them quotable material, a way to get in touch for an interview, and a sample of the product if applicable.

48

PRODUCT LAUNCH GUIDANCE

LET'S SEND THIS ROCKET TO THE MOON!

I have been involved in many product launches and service launches over the last 25 years. For that matter, I've been involved in multiple company launches. I've also been a part of several product launches on Kickstarter. All of these except one did quite well and went well beyond the goal. The secret to a successful launch can be boiled down to one word - preparation. That is no great insight, and it's pretty obvious that poor preparation leads to poor results, so let's look at what it takes to prepare for a launch and when to start.

I've already mentioned that for a complex electronics product there were nearly 18 months of time from idea to crowdfunding. For the wallet, there were about nine months. For other products I was involved with the time from concept to Kickstarter varied between three months and two years. But some of that time was spent developing the product - so let's say you are already at the prototype phase, how long does it take to plan a product launch? Here again, I have to say that the range varies. I have had companies I work with make a prototype and within 30 days have all the marketing assets, the website, videos, email copy, and lists of potential customers ready to go. But to get to that, there was a Product Development Team of a dozen people working full time. Other products with much smaller teams took 3-6 months.

Working with at least a product development specialist, or preferably a team, who has worked on multiple products in the past, will help make the product launch successful. The more familiar that team is with what will need to go into your product launch, the more likely they will hit deadlines and deliver a good launch campaign. Note: I don't say more likely your product will be a success, because you can have a great product team, get everything done right, and then face a lack of product acceptance in the marketplace. Unfortunately, sometimes products fail even if all indicators are that they should succeed. Having an experienced team will help prevent missteps along the way, but it is not a guarantee of product success.

Launching a product successfully requires the alignment of a lot of unrelated events. Sometimes you get lucky and occasionally lousy luck robs you of success. A good product launch consultant will be able to make sure that as many things as can be controlled are, and that as many potential obstacles are avoided as possible. Knowing how holidays in China will affect product shipment, where to use paid advertising, and how far in advance, how to get free or paid endorsements, and how to create a sense of urgency in the product team are all skills a great product launch specialist will have. Their job is much like a producer, to interact with a lot of moving parts and be sure the whole process proceeds smoothly.

Finding the right person for this role is not easy because there are not many people with experience in this specialized field, so if you want to get expert help for your product launch, allow for three to six months before launch to find the right person or team to make the launch go smoothly. Doing so will increase your odds of success.

V

CONCLUSION

49

A WORD ABOUT COACHES AND CONSULTANTS

*I*n this book, I have used the word consultant in almost every chapter. This is not by accident as one of the themes of this book is to remind you, as the CEO or owner of a business that you should look outside your immediate staff to find temporary experts who can guide you through specialized aspects of growing your business. Consultants are experts who have manyfold experience doing something that you may be doing for the first time in your company, or something that you have tried to do on your own unsuccessfully. The people who are consultants are generally not needed by the company on a permanent basis, nor are they usually affordable beyond short, specific projects.

But there is another type of person who often works with business owners or executives who is entirely different from a consultant. That person is a Business Coach. There is a difference between people who are consultants and people who are business coaches, so let me tell you why I think there is a significant differences.

I started working for companies on a contract basis to help them fix their computers while I was in college in 1990. Technically, I guess I started in high school, but the first independent jobs I had where I came in to fix computers were in college. I got a taste of what consulting was - short term, addressing the needs of the client by doing something they could not do themselves and explaining to them what it is that I did, and why. My friends were delivering Domino's Pizza for $4.50/hr while I was working with companies charging $40/hr for my computer services.

After college, I got my first full-time job as an IT manager for a small business. There I was paid a salary of $30,000 a year and expected to do anything the company needed relating to computers or networks. When I had needs beyond my own skills, I could request that a consultant come in and help. There I got a taste for what it meant to be an employee.

I liked being a consultant more. It offered not only much higher hourly pay but more flexibility of where I worked and what I did. I also noticed it garnered much more respect. If I came in to help a company with their computers, they listened to me much more attentively than their internal employees, even though I may have been 15 years younger and much less experienced. I discovered the advantage of an outside perspective.

Most people trust the advice of a friend more than a stranger, but they also place a higher value on the opinion of a stranger because it is unbiased. David Dunning, of the Dunning–Kruger Effect fame, has conducted studies that show an illogically higher trust in the authoritativeness of strangers. This helps to explain why employees very often show frustration at their companies ignoring suggestions for improvements from employees, only to act on identical suggestions when received from consultants. This effect is real in my experience. In fact, I now tell employees during my interviews with them that I will very likely recommend that the company do something which has already been suggested internally. I explain to them that my job is to help the company improve, not to take credit for the suggestions, so I ask them for such suggestions so that proper credit can be given if they are later implemented. I do this because I do not need to bolster my ego, but also because I'm a firm believer in efficiency - if suggestions from employees for improvement can point me in the right direction for the focus of my own research, then I'm ahead of the curve. If that research confirms the employee suggestion, then when I present recommendations to the owner or executives, I mention that an employee had already made this suggestion.

Thus far, I've been speaking about psychology more than consulting or coaches. This is because I wanted to set the stage for that conversation and so you keep in mind that people have a bias to place a higher value on advice from strangers more than associates. As I defined previously, consultants help a business do something it does not have the knowledge and resources to do internally and set the example for the way the company should do this function in the future. The key here is that a Consultant is someone who can do the role that no one in the business can do at the level of the consultant. They are an expert in their field, much as a

Priest is an expert in the Bible, or a Lawyer is an expert in Law. Consultants are practitioner subject matter experts. This means they practice their trade and have the ability to either explain to others what they should be doing, or step into that role and execute.

Now let's look at coaches. I have observed the rise of business coaching over the last 30 years. My earliest experiences were with a Psychotherapist friend who was getting bored of her job and decided to become a CEO coach in 1993. She had a Ph.D. She understood human psychology and how motivation works. She worked with CEOs to help them focus stress and deal better with business problems. I thought back then that a better approach to the problem was simply to hire better CEOs! Yes, I'm kidding here, a bit.

Now, fast forward 25 years, and there are more business coaches than you can throw a stick at. Search for business coaching and your browser will be inundated with paid ads for business coaching "schools" which will offer a piece of paper with metallic stamps for anywhere from $25-$2,500. You can study your way, in just a few hours, to becoming a person from whom CEOs should take advice. There is a multitude of books in the Amazon Top 100 with titles promoting better income through becoming a business coach. Hundreds of millions of dollars have been made by companies selling promises of becoming business coaches. In a nutshell, the value of the term coach in the business context has now gone through the toilet. For many people, the term coach in an email ranks similarly with pyramid and Viagra. We can thank the coaching schools for this. The term has stayed the same, the misappropriation of it for "get rich with little work" programs has ruined it.

So what did a coach mean and how is it different from a consultant? Well a coach, other than the thing that people sit on and is propelled by a horse, is someone whose job is to help the person they are working with achieve the desired result though encouragement, suggestions, and ideas the person would not have come up with on their own. A coach helps a person feel like she is not alone in working toward a goal. If you ever had a math tutor or were a math tutor, then you know a tutor's job was not to provide answers, but to help the student figure out how to best come up with the solutions themselves. A tutor could be someone taking the same class at the same time as the student. A coach is very similar. A coach does not have to be an expert because their job is not to provide the right answer but rather to help the client figure out the answer on their own. For the most part, a coach is not an expert and absolutely can not do the job of the CEO or other senior executives. The coach can motivate and encourage.

When I hired a personal trainer to help me work out and lose weight, I did not look for someone who was once out of shape and then lost weight. I looked for someone who could help with suggestions about exercise, who would encourage me when I was doing well, and help me getting back on track when I fell off the wagon. This is a coaching role. This is a valid, useful role in providing support for someone who is doing the actual work of weight loss. This is not a weight loss consultant.

So this is where it gets muddy. Most consultants can act as

coaches. They are subject matter experts who can provide advice to their clients who want to make their own decisions. But they are also fully capable of making decisions and executing on them on behalf of the client. In a nutshell, a consultant is someone who can do the work, or discuss the work, while a coach is someone who may not be able to do the job, for whatever reason, but can review the work with the client.

Sometimes a coach is someone who used to be a consultant, but retired and decided that they no longer want the stress of actually managing people or projects and merely want to give advice. This would be akin to a lawyer who no longer practices law, but can still provide anecdotal advice. There is a use for that kind of relationship, but hiring a lawyer who does not practice law is exactly like hiring a coach as a consultant.

If you want someone to figure out how to help you brainstorm about how you are dealing with problems, a coach can do that. But if you want someone to actually solve your problems, then you need a consultant. And if you are interested in merely having someone to talk to about your problems, then you need a psychotherapist. How does that make you feel? Sorry, couldn't resist going back to my first reference of a coach. (Ha!)

There is a place for business coaching. Unfortunately, the "Business of Coaching" industry has worked very hard to sell the idea of coaching as something synonymous with consulting. After all, would you pay for the advice on your marketing campaign to someone who has never done marketing for anyone else, but went to "Marketing Coaching School?" Or would you pay more to someone who can do your marketing for you and has done marketing for others? I know I'm throwing a lot of analogies out here to make my point about the distinction between coaching and consulting, but right now that definition is so muddled in business books and press that many people think that the terms are synonymous with each other. They are not.

50

NOW WHAT?

*T*his chapter is at the end of the book because this book is for people who read it and absorb the information, not the casual skimmers who will skip sections and flip through the rest of the book. If you're this far by reading or listening to the book, then you indeed are the person I was writing this book for, regardless of whether you run a $25 million company or if you aspire to one day.

This book is for the business owner who will recognize many of the issues covered in the book and hopefully find some guidance for getting past them. As I mentioned in the Preface, by including so many different issues I've helped companies overcome, I've had to provide a high-level overview to keep the length of the book reasonable. For some, this will be enough to get their creative juices flowing and flush out the solution to a similar problem in their own company. For those who need more guidance, go ahead and contact me. The details are below.

However, I also recognize that not everyone reading this

book founded a company. Some of you may be running companies you did not start! You may be an employee right now but have ambitions of having your own company someday. You may be a student reading a stolen PDF file of this book (I know who you are!) Or you may be the crazy person like me who likes to read business books for fun. For anyone who did not recognize themselves as the subject of this book, I challenge you to internalize the lessons of this book!

Anyone can become more than they think they can. I believe, everyone at any level of achievement can still achieve more. Without getting too motivational sounding, please know that if you have a company of one, or even if you are working for someone else and are just dreaming of starting your own business someday, this book is still for you. In fact, you may get more out of it than someone who is already running a multi-million dollar company because you are in a position to navigate all the gotchas and issues by reading this book! I only ask that you let me know when you have a growing successful business and tell me about how much I have helped you!

It is a bit of a cliché to say that the only thing holding you back is you, but it is unquestionably true of the most intelligent people I have met over the last 25 years. People with talent always assume they have less talent than they do. People with honed skills always believe everyone else is just as skilled. People with the best ideas often don't speak up, because they assume others have better ideas. This is not modesty; this is an intelligence perception flaw. By being above average intelligence, you misapply baseline intelligence that you have yourself to everyone else. It's like having 20/20 vision and not realizing that very few people actually have that while most people need glasses or contacts to see that well. So in a convoluted roundabout way, I'm trying to say that if you read this book, you are more likely to be someone who overestimated the success of others and underestimated your own potential for success.

Let me be one more voice to say that you are more capable than you think you are. The main thing stopping you from achieving more in any part of your life is the Über-Ich. If you can get past your own belief system, you can set your mind free to achieve greater success.

Contact

I absolutely want to hear from readers of this book. I will do my best to reply to every message.

If you see yourself in some of the stories and want help growing your company, please contact me and I will let you know how I can help.

You can contact me through the contact form at my company website: www.companyoverhaul.com

Or email: books@naftulyev.com

IF YOU CONNECT with me on Facebook, fair warning: I only login once a week and do not post much.

YOU CAN ALSO SEND me a message on LinkedIn, but please keep in mind that I have a rule for LinkedIn connections that we must have met in person. I have over 1000 connections there, most of whom are CxO level people.